ZERO HOUR

and Other Documentary Poems

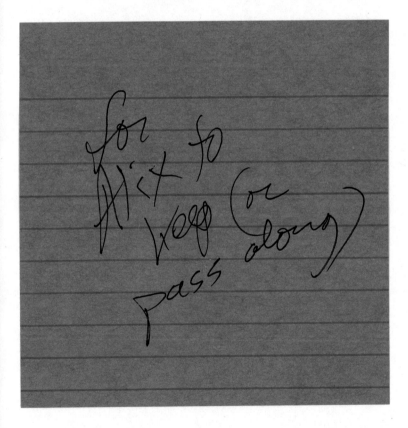

Ernesto Cardenal
ZERO HOUR
and Other Documentary Poems

Selected and edited by Donald D. Walsh,
with an introductory essay by Robert Pring-Mill

Translations by Paul W. Borgeson, Jr., Jonathan Cohen,
Robert Pring-Mill, and Donald D. Walsh

A NEW DIRECTIONS BOOK

The original Spanish-language texts of the poems included in this vol-
ume: © Casa de las Américas, 1979; © Ediciones Sígueme, 1976; © 1974,
1976, Ernesto Cardenal; © Barral Editores, S. A.–Barcelona, 1974; ©
Carlos Lohé, soc. anón. ind. y com., 1971, 1973

"Lights" was originally published as a broadside by The Black Hole
School of Poethnics. "Trip to New York" first appeared in Sun.

Manufactured in the United States of America
First published clothbound and as New Directions Paperbook 502 in 1980
Published simultaneously in Canada by Penguin Books Canada Limited

Library of Congress Cataloging in Publication Data

Cardenal, Ernesto.
    Zero hour and other documentary poems.
    (A New Directions Book)
    CONTENTS: Walsh, D. D. Preface.—Pring-Mill, R. The
redemption of reality through documentary poetry.—Zero
hour.—Nicaraguan canto. [etc.]
    I. Walsh, Donald Devenish, 1903–1980 II. Title.
PQ7519.C034A22   1980   861   80–36817
ISBN 0–8112–0766–8
ISBN 0–8112–0767–6 (pbk.)

New Directions Books are published for James Laughlin
by New Directions Publishing Corporation,
80 Eighth Avenue, New York 10011

SECOND PRINTING

CONTENTS

PREFACE

Ernesto Cardenal is a Catholic priest and a Marxist poet, and he sees no conflict between these two loyalties. Born in 1925 in Granada, Nicaragua, he studied at the University of Mexico (1943–47) and Columbia University (1947–49), where he was deeply influenced by the poetry of Ezra Pound. From 1957 to 1959 he was a novice at the Trappist Monastery at Gethsemani, Kentucky, where his spiritual director was Thomas Merton. They came to know and to translate each other's poetry.

The rigors of the Trappist training were too great for Cardenal's fragile health, but he did spend the years 1959 to 1965 studying for the priesthood, and he was ordained in 1965. At the urging of Merton, he returned to Nicaragua and established a church and commune which he named Nuestra Señora de Solentiname. Solentiname is an archipelago of thirty-eight islands on Lake Nicaragua, with a population of a thousand *campesinos* and fishermen. Sunday services at Solentiname focused on readings from the Gospels and on the vocal (at times very vocal) reactions of the congregation to the readings. These are now appearing in translation.*

In 1970 Cardenal was invited to Cuba to be a judge in a poetry contest conducted by the Casa de las Américas. He stayed three months and wrote a book on his generally enthusiastic reactions to Castro's Cuba.**

In 1977 appeared *Apocalypse and Other Poems,* a collection of Cardenal's short poetry from the 1940s to 1973, including, among others, "Epigrams," "Prayer for Marilyn Monroe," "Coplas on the Death of Merton," "Recordings of the Sacred Pipe," "Condensations," and the title poem.***

In October 1977, the Nicaraguan government, then under the Somoza dictatorship, exasperated beyond endurance by the intensifi-

---

* *The Gospel in Solentiname.* 4 vols. Tr. Donald D. Walsh. Orbis Books. 1976–80.
** *In Cuba.* Tr. Donald D. Walsh. New Directions. 1974.
*** Edited by Robert Pring-Mill and Donald D. Walsh. New Directions.

cation of revolutionist activity in Solentiname, ordered the destruction of the commune. Forced into exile, Cardenal became a roving ambassador for the FSLN (Frente Sandinista de Liberación Nacional), the guerrilla group that in 1979 toppled Somoza. Cardenal was named Minister of Culture in the new government.

Although the poems in the present volume were written between 1954 and 1979, they are as timely and as timeless as dictatorship and police brutality on any continent and in any country. In addition, they are heart-breaking and heart-warming poetry.

Madison, Connecticut   D. D.W.

THE REDEMPTION OF REALITY
THROUGH DOCUMENTARY POETRY

James Monaco's *How to Read a Film* is surprisingly helpful when read-
ing the "documentary poetry" of Ernesto Cardenal, the well-known
Nicaraguan poet-priest: what Monaco has to say about the foremost
theorist of film realism—Siegfried Kracauer—fits Cardenal precisely,
if one just reads "poetry" for "film" throughout. In Kracauer's case,
film

> serves a purpose. It does not exist simply for itself, as a pure esthetic
> object; it exists in the context of the world around it. Since it stems
> from reality it must also return to it—hence the subtitle [of Kracauer's
> *Theory of Film*]: *The Redemption of Physical Reality*. If this sounds
> vaguely religious, the connotation is, I think, intended. For Kracauer,
> film has a human, ethical nature. Ethics must replace esthetics,
> thereby fulfilling Lenin's prophecy . . . that "ethics are the esthetics
> of the future." . . . [We] need the redemption [which] film offers:
> we need to be brought back into communication with the physical
> world. Film can mediate reality for us. It can both "corroborate" and
> "debunk" our impressions of reality.[1]

All Cardenal's poetry "debunks," "corroborates," and "mediates" re-
ality. His esthetic principles are clearly ethical, and most of his poems
are more than just "vaguely" religious. But the filmic parallel fits the
"documentary poems" of the present collection particularly well,
though I am not trying to suggest that Cardenal has ever gone to the
films in a conscious search for fresh techniques.

   The poetry of his first New Directions collection, *Apocalypse and
Other Poems* (1977), used a wide variety of styles and ranged in
length from lapidary epigrams to extended evocations of primitive
Amerindian cultures—often with much use of Poundian collage
techniques and vivid imagery. But all eight texts of *Zero Hour and
Other Documentary Poems* set out to "document" reality (and so re-
deem it) in a more dialectically visual way: picturing things, peoples,
and events in the light of a clear-cut sociopolitical commitment; select-
ing, shaping, and imposing interpretative patterns on the world, with
liberal use of such filmic "editing" techniques as crosscutting, accel-
erated montage, or flash frames; and pursuing "the redemption of
physical reality" by bringing us "back into communication" with its

harshness and its beauty. Poets and cameras can both affect what they record, but whereas a documentary camera's presence conditions the "on-going situation," Cardenal's recording of the present or the past is aimed at helping to shape the future—involving the reader in the poetic process in order to provoke him into full political commitment, thus fostering the translation of the poet's more prophetic visions into sociopolitical fact.

The label "documentary poems" is mine not his, but Cardenal seemed pleased with it when I coined it in 1972 in order to highlight the features which distinguished "Zero Hour" (composed in 1954–56) and "Nicaraguan Canto" (1970–72) from the kinds of poetry on which *Apocalypse* was to draw. It suits "Mosquito Kingdom" (1972), "Oracle over Managua" (1972–73) and "Trip to New York" (1973), and also fits the two "Epistles" (one sent "to Monsignor Casaldáliga" in 1974, and one "to José Coronel Urtecho" in 1975), although their titles underline the fusion of an earlier "biblical" mode with his more recent documentary approach. Those seven poems are fairly long: even the shortest—"Mosquito Kingdom"—runs to almost two hundred lines, while "Oracle over Managua" is just short of a thousand. The eighth poem, "Lights" (1979), is also a documentary, but a far shorter one, brought in by way of epilogue because it describes Cardenal's return to Nicaragua from exile, after the fall of Somoza in July 1979.

None of the longer poems is simple, though they all aim at surface clarity, being meant for a wide public. They are strictly "factual," but facts can be double-edged, and their juxtapositions can also set up further meanings. Cardenal's reader cannot just sit back and "listen" to the words and rhythm: he has to visualize sequences of disparate images (each one a snatched glimpse of reality), noting their pairings and progressions, matching them both with each other and with what is left unsaid—and thereby sharing in the extraction of their fuller "meaning." These poems demand more than just an alert response, because the poet wishes to prod us beyond thought and into action: his texts are never just concerned to document and understand reality, but also to help change it—which is why they have been called "The Poetry of Useful Prophecy."[2] But the data have to be recorded before reality can be reshaped, and the reshaping lies beyond the poems themselves: the changes for which the poet yearns lie in the future.

To be precise, those changes all lay in the future when these poems were written, but many of his prophecies are now being translated into fact by the Nicaraguan Revolution. Their poet, who wrote "Zero Hour" back in the 1950s against the first Somoza to tyrannize Nicaragua and who was to become—two decades later—the spokesman of the liberation movement which brought the last Somoza down, returned from exile as Minister of Culture in the Nicaraguan Government of Reconstruction, and the cultural values which he now promotes are clearly stated in the later poems of this collection. Neither those values nor the realities which his poetry tries to redeem are of purely local relevance, yet the poetry must be viewed in its original context for its wider implications to emerge.

When *Apocalypse* appeared in 1977, Cardenal was living quietly in Nuestra Señora de Solentiname, a religious commune on a remote tropical island in the Great Lake of Nicaragua. After revolutionary activism in the 1950s—reflected in the last part of "Zero Hour"—he had renounced violence, under Merton's influence. Having tried his vocation at the Trappist Abbey of Gethsemani in Kentucky, where Merton was the novice-master, he completed his training as a Roman Catholic priest in Mexico and Colombia. Ordained in August 1965, at the age of thirty, he founded the Solentiname commune with two friends in 1966. There, he continued to preach Mertonian nonviolence for many years, while studies of the high pre-Columbian cultures and the beliefs and rituals of primitive Amerindian tribes—both vividly reflected in the poems of *Homage to the American Indians*[3]—had deepened his respect for the peaceful spiritual values he discerned in the premilitary society of the Classic Mayan cities, as well as in the classless systems of those tribes. Their values largely coincided with those of the early church, and he recreated them in his own commune, most of whose later members were Nicaraguan *campesinos*.

For eleven years, it remained a tranquil haven in a violent land: Nicaragua had been ruled by the Somoza family since the mid-1930s, and though the first dictator—Anastasio ("Tacho") Somoza—was killed in 1956 by a lone patriot, control remained in the hands of the Somozas or their nominees. By 1977, Tacho's second son—"Tachito"—had been directly or indirectly in power for a whole decade. Supported by the United States as a bulwark against communism, as well as by American big business—Tachito had a powerful lobby on his side in Washington—Nicaragua's third Somoza headed one of the most oppressive regimes in Latin America. Meanwhile, and chiefly inspired by the Cuban Revolution, a guerrilla movement known as the FSLN (the Frente Sandinista de Liberación Nacional, or Sandinista National Liberation Front) came into being in the early 1960s, taking its name from the *guerrillero* general Augusto César Sandino who had been murdered in 1934 on the orders of the first Somoza. Sandino is the hero of the second episode of "Zero Hour," and the many parallels between the guerrilla warfare of the FSLN and Sandino's earlier war against the American marines underpin the structure of "Nicaraguan Canto," which Cardenal dedicated "to the FSLN" when it was first published "underground" in July 1972; but he was still preaching a peaceful social revolution when I went to spend that summer with him in Solentiname, though the pressures toward violence were already mounting.

Most of the Catholic hierarchy still sided with the interests of the ruling class throughout Latin America, but the "theology of liberation" had been gaining ground among the younger priests. Some of them—such as the Colombian university chaplain Camilo Torres—had even given up their ministry to join guerrilla groups. We talked a lot about Camilo Torres, whose decision Cardenal openly admired although he said that he himself could never take up arms, and it was clear that he had already moved well to the left of the majority of "progressive" Roman Catholic theologians of liberation. He had been deeply influenced by three months spent in Cuba in 1970, which persuaded him that many reforms he had deemed unattainable could be achieved in practice, though not without an equally radical restructuring of the social order. The prose work *In Cuba* (his first volume published by New Directions, in 1974) describes that visit vividly. Part of its attraction lies in the naïve directness of its reporting, and it comments with appealing frankness on certain obvious Cuban faults, but what captured his imagination was the basic concept of Cuba's "New Society," with its puritanical morality (in striking contrast to the decadent aspects of Western society which he had so often attacked) and an egalitarian work ethic which appeared to offer a viable alternative to capitalist private enterprise.

At his request, I checked the first printed copy of the Spanish text (*En Cuba*, 1972) for errata (and there were many, since no Buenos Aires printing could be adequately supervised from distant Solentiname). We also talked a lot about his Cuban experience, and I summed up his attitude as follows in my introduction to *Apocalypse*:

While noting that the system had its faults, the only thing it seemed to him to lack to be a viable replacement for capitalist society was a sound Christian basis. If its drastic changes in the social order—in the here-and-now of life-on-earth—could but be grounded in theological principles which look[ed] beyond this world to a timeless reality, then lasting social justice would be achieved. The New People "that is going to be born" would be a people made up of the New Men whom Che Guevara predicated, but the values of their "communism" would coincide with those of the earliest Christians.

It is important for our understanding of his changing attitudes that both that text and an earlier study (where the same point was made at greater length) were submitted to Cardenal—in 1975 and 1977—and met with no dissent. Yet when I spent long hours with him in Costa Rica in July 1979, just before the final triumph of the Sandinistas, he said that I had been mistaken in thinking that he had ever felt the Cuban system lacked a Christian grounding, because he had *always* thought it "was a truly Christian society already." Having myself just come from Cuba, and having seen how the practice of Christianity normally proved a barrier to all advancement, I must confess that I found this view of Cuba as an ideal Christian state disquietingly naïve. But this was certainly how *he* saw Cuba during our talks in July 1979. What he said made me realize that many a statement in the later "documentary poems" which I had taken to be either evangelical exaggeration or "poetic license" was meant to be taken strictly at face value.

Even in 1972, it was clear that he had already begun to modify the Mertonian ideal of strict nonviolence (albeit with great reluctance), having come to recognize that existing structures were unlikely to be changed by peaceful means; but by July 1979 he had moved so far from his Mertonian stance that he could champion violence as the sword of divine justice, and even preach the virtues of a Holy War. I suppose that the first signs of this great shift in attitude had been there for me to read in 1972, had I had "eyes to see" or "ears to hear": the spiritual life of Solentiname already revolved round the kind of collective discussion of scriptural texts which later produced the printed dialogues of *The Gospel in Solentiname*,[4] and many of the texts were glossed in a highly revolutionary way. The revolutionary form of Roman Catholicism which these discussions embody is likely to flourish in much of Latin America, however much the Vatican may try to prevent any further radicalization of the Catholic church in the Third World.

Its ideas are relevant to all except the earliest of these eight "documentary poems": "Zero Hour" (a Latin American revolutionary classic for over twenty years) was written during his *first* militant phase—before his religious conversion—whereas all the others are subsequent to his experience of Cuba, which he has frequently described as being "almost a second conversion." Today, the period of fourteen nonviolent years between those two "conversions" seems no more than a pacific interlude in a predominantly militant career.

Yet how exactly was it that the mounting pressure of events in Nicaragua came to shatter the peace of the commune he had founded under Merton's guidance, leading him into exile and the gospel of a Holy War? First came a major natural disaster: the earthquake which destroyed the center of Managua on December 23, 1972, killing perhaps as many as fifteen thousand people. It produced a surge of international aid, but as much as fifty percent of this found its way into the pockets of Somoza, his relatives and business cronies, and the officers of his National Guard—Tachito having failed to appreciate the extent to which the cynical flagrancy of such post-quake corruption would foster discontent at every level of his people. Cardenal's "Oracle over Managua" is a meditation on the aftermath of the catastrophe, while "Trip to New York" records a six-day journey which he made in June 1973, to help raise funds for the survivors.

Mounting criticism of the regime strengthened the position of the FSLN, and its increased activities in the northern hills led to mass killings of *campesinos* by the National Guard, in an attempt to cut off its supplies. Cardenal's first "Epistle" was composed against this background, when he was asked to preface a collection of poems called *Tierra nuestra, libertad* by Mgr. Pedro María Casaldáliga (Bishop of São Felix, in the Brazilian Matto Grosso): a sorrowful poem, full of indignation at the immensity of human anguish in their respective countries, yet heartened by the poet's sense of Christian solidarity (for "there where the helicopters gather is the Body of Christ").

His second "Epistle" was an open letter to an old friend and mentor, the Nicaraguan poet José Coronel Urtecho, written as the quality of life in Nicaragua grew steadily worse, and published in Spain (in 1976) in a volume of Cardenal's writings whose title means *The Sanctity of Revolution*.[5] Soon afterward words became deeds, when the FSLN made its first unsuccessful attempt to bring about a popular uprising, in October 1977. Its failure meant the end of the Solentiname commune: by then, the small community had become virtually an FSLN cell, and most of its younger members joined in a fairly successful attack on the National Guard garrison at San Carlos, an inland port at the head of the Río San Juan (in the southeastern corner of Lake Nicaragua). When an airstrike heralded the arrival of reinforcements, they were obliged to withdraw across the jungle border into Costa Rica.

Cardenal had left some days before, to represent the FSLN abroad. Reprisals for the San Carlos raid were brutal, including the detention and removal of most of the remaining islanders (many of whom just "disappeared" in custody) and the destruction of every building at Nuestra Señora de Solentiname except the church, which was used as a temporary barracks. Outlawed by Somoza, Cardenal published an open letter about the assault on San Carlos and the consequent destruction of his community, soon followed by a separate statement proudly proclaiming himself an active member of the Sandinistas. His "Open Letter to the People of Nicaragua" said that collective meditation on the social relevance of scripture had played the leading part in the radicalization of his commune, ultimately inspiring its members to join in the armed struggle "for one reason alone: out of their love for the kingdom of God. Out of their ardent desire to establish a just society, a true and concrete kingdom of God here on this earth."[6]

After 1977, events moved increasingly swiftly in Nicaragua. The murder of Pedro Joaquín Chamorro (the chief opposition leader, and editor of *La Prensa*) led to a general strike, in January 1978. An uprising in Masaya—near the capital—was savagely put down in early March, with the destruction of the Indian quarter of Monimbó and the massacre of several hundred of its inhabitants. Toward the end of August, the FSLN led a more general uprising in fifteen towns, but the National Guard succeeded in re-establishing a precarious control over most of the country after several weeks, at the cost of between six thousand and ten thousand lives (chiefly civilians, killed in massive airstrikes as well as in the reprisals which followed the recapture of each rebellious town).

After withdrawing into the hills in order to regroup, the FSLN consolidated its three politically somewhat diverse sections into a single fighting force, which launched a third and decisive offensive in May 1979, just after the beginning of the rainy season. Faced by its military success, the United States abandoned Somoza just seven weeks later, and he fled the country on July 17.

That morning, I was wakened in my hotel room in San José by a very early call from Cardenal, asking whether I had heard the news: "*Se fue*—he's gone—*Somoza ya se fue. . . .*" But those final weeks of fighting had claimed perhaps another thirty thousand Nicaraguan lives and left close to a quarter of a million people homeless (about a seventh of the country's total population). Only a day after Somoza's resignation, the new government was flown into Nicaragua by night, under conditions of great secrecy vividly described by Cardenal in

"Lights"—the first poem he had written since leaving Solentiname just over nineteen months before, and the last one in this collection.

Whether Cardenal will be able to write much poetry while Minister of Culture seems doubtful, particularly since his accustomed method of composition involves long periods of meditation: drafting, redrafting, cutting up, and re-assembling numerous versions, on the way toward the final process of montage (often working on several poems in parallel, with the composition of the longer ones sometimes lasting over several years). He told me in San José, just after his appointment to his ministerial post, that he could see no way to get back to this kind of work till he could withdraw from public politics, adding that he could not write poetry in any other way. He hoped to be able to refound Nuestra Señora de Solentiname, "but on a far wider base, as a center sponsoring the development of popular culture throughout the *campesinos* of Nicaragua." Meanwhile, there is the literacy campaign to be promoted and seen through (it is being co-ordinated by Ernesto's brother Fernando, a Jesuit). All his ideals for the raising of consciousness which this campaign will foster will be found, clearly voiced, at different points in these eight documentary poems.

Out of the eight, the one which offers a United States reader the easiest point of entry is probably the fifth, the 1973 "Trip to New York": its environment is familiar, the attitudes it documents (and many of the people named) will be familiar to readers of New Directions books, and this account of a rushed six-day trip is the closest thing in any of the longer poems to the direct reporting of immediate experience, as in a personal diary. It ought to be read, however, as a deliberately "public" diary, and also *strictly as poetry*: its appearance of uncommitted objectivity is a studied one, achieving its effects (as almost always in his better poems) obliquely, by poetic means—although its "images" *are* real, not metaphorical. They may seem as clear and as immediately revealed as snapshots taken with a Polaroid camera—photos which materialize "before one's very eyes," often still in the presence of the objects photographed (in "real life") against which one is able to control the degree of "likeness" which the camera has captured. But readers cannot match these shots against what they depict, and they have all been carefully selected and assembled (just as one ought, indeed, to "edit" one's vacation slides before inflicting them on friends!). The process is less intellectual than intuitive: when pressed to say *how* he selects which details of "reality" to represent, Cardenal can never rationalize his procedure, saying no more than that he "knows" which details will turn out to be "poetic" in a given context. The shots he uses are, naturally, "angled" (so are a camera's): taken from the poet's individual viewpoint, which always has inherent ethical and moral preoccupations. They have been chosen and grouped (however intuitively) with a sure sense for thematic links and quiet ironies—some of which the poet makes explicit, but not all. Thus it would be rather naïve to take "Trip to New York" as no more than a simple diary, or a piece of instant reportage couched in free verse.

Readers would do well to examine Cardenal's methods in the familiar context of that known environment before they move into the half-alien Latin American world of the remaining poems, the first of which—"Zero Hour" ("Hora O" or "La hora cero")—is certainly the best-known of all his longer poems. As it is also the one which displays many of his favorite techniques in their most graspable form, it merits examination at somewhat greater length by way of introduction to the much later series of post-Cuban documentary poems. "Zero Hour" is in four parts: a brief opening section, in the nature of an introit, establishing the mood of Central American life under dictatorships, followed by three separate episodes. The first one concerns the economic factors underlying the politics of "banana republics"; the second is about Sandino, culminating in his treacherous execution (along with his brother Sócrates and two of his own commanders) on Tacho's orders, within three weeks of peace having been signed; while the third concerns the Conspiración de Abril, an anti-Somozan plot which misfired (in April 1954), in which Cardenal himself took part.

The first episode, largely based on data taken from a book called *El imperio del banano,* was written in 1954. The overlapping composition of the other two came later, the second being based on various documentary sources, while the third grew out of Cardenal's own notes—made soon after the event, but reworked into poetry over a period of about two years. The "introit" was actually the last part to be written, not being composed till after Cardenal's religious conversion in 1956, and it ends with his earliest use of a Biblical quotation in the actual body of a poem:

> Watchman! What hour is it of the night?
> Watchman! What hour is it of the night?

taken from *Isaiah* (21:11). The unstated but implied "How long, oh Lord, how long?" is typical of his oblique approach. So, too, is the stylistic equivalent of a "throwaway remark" in lines like

> "Often while smoking a cigarette
> I've decided that a man should die,"
> says Ubico smoking a cigarette . . .

in which the symbolic juxtaposition of speech with a visual detail which would be quite innocent without the speech creates a chilling filmic image.

The whole introit depends on swiftly effective contrasts, whose "meaning" is not spoilt by being spelled out: the Guatemalan dictator with "a head cold," while his people are dispersed with phosphorous bombs; a single window of the Honduran dictator's office smashed, provoking an inappropriately violent response from armed police. Such introductory "shots" build up the setting and its atmosphere in the same terms and ways as does the opening sequence of almost any film. Other techniques which will recur in the three episodes. Thus the collage of documentary sources in the "economic" sequence, with its oppressive and depersonalizing lists of company names and alienating juxtapositions of contrastive factual details, will become a characteristically Cardenalian technique (one learned from Pound, and which has influenced many younger Spanish American poets through its use by Cardenal). Equally characteristic are the shafts of irony, often dependent on the reversal of an expected phrase—like "Carías is the dictator/who didn't build the greatest number of miles of railroad" (in Honduras).

The Sandino episode brings in many favorite themes: heroic self-abnegation, the purity of motives, and the egalitarian virtues of a guerrilla force "more like a community than like an army/and more united by love than by military discipline"—features he will all use much later as heroic precedents, when depicting the Sandinista *guerrilleros* of the following generation. At one stage, he punctuates the action with repeated snatches of "Adelita" (perhaps the favorite song of the 1910 Mexican Revolution), intensifying the vision of Sandino's forces as a "happy army" since "A love song was its battle hymn." This is a typically filmic use of song. Filmic, too, is the accelerated montage of the death sequence, with its visual and aural crosscutting between parallel actions: the exchanges between Somoza and the American minister (and later between the American minister and Moncada) punctuated by the digging of a grave, a glimpse of prisoners, and the halting of Sandino's car, whose unnamed passengers are hustled off to face the firing squad.

Similar devices are used in the third episode. Cardenal's own entry on the scene intensifies the mood ("I was with them in the April rebellion/and I learned how to handle a Rising machine gun"). Its effect is—characteristically—heightened by the lack of further elaboration, as the "I-was-there" device gives way to the stark understatement of the hunting down and slaughter of Adolfo Báez Bone, whose identification with the land in which his body lies ensures his resurrection in the collective body of his people (a theme which becomes a leitmotif in later poems). The lyrical use of landscape and the seasons to echo or contrast with man's affairs—a striking feature of both the second and the third episodes—is a device which will achieve even greater prominence in "Nicaraguan Canto," the "Oracle," and both "Epistles."

An understanding of how "Zero Hour" establishes its points helps greatly with later poems, where the chronological sequence of events is deliberately dislocated by abrupt (but often unspecified) temporal intercutting, while the poetic texture is complicated by far greater use of understated or oblique "symbolic images"—or brief references whose wider connotations only emerge with hindsight, like the thrush which "sings/in freedom, in the North" (in the first few lines of "Nicaraguan Canto"): an unstated echo of Sandino, later to be revealed as the first hint of the presence of contemporary Sandinista freedom fighters in the same Northern hills. "Nicaraguan Canto" (whose Spanish title—*Canto Nacional*—is as much a Nerudian as a Poundian echo) culminates in one of Cardenal's most startling *tours de force*: its last nine lines consist entirely of birdsong—not a device which any translator could hope to reproduce with much success.

After the "Canto," "Mosquito Kingdom" (*"Reino mosco"*) provides easier reading, starting with the factual parody of Western pomp at the drunken coronation of a black British-sponsored puppet king as nominal ruler of the scattered nineteenth-century British settlements along the Mosquito Coast (all the way from Belize to Costa Rica), peopled by English-speaking former slaves from the West Indies, the Miskito Indians themselves, and the mixed race born of their intermarriage. The poem jumps forward in time to the pompous ostentation of Cornelius Vanderbilt's huge private yacht *North Star* and Vanderbilt's involvement in the attempted exploitation of that Caribbean coast, and then cuts to a series of sordid and ill-fated dealings among its actual or would-be exploiters. Although the obscurity of this facet of nineteenth-century Nicaraguan local history may puzzle foreign readers, there is no missing the point of Cardenal's satirical devices.

"Oracle over Managua" (*"Oráculo sobre Managua"*) is a more somber and a far more complex poem. The earthquake which destroyed the city in 1972 is merely the latest stage of a long geological process, and the poem harks back to the long-past eruption which recorded the feet of fleeing prehistoric men and beasts in a layer of volcanic mud which later turned to stone, out at Acahualinca: the site of one of the worst of the shanty-towns which fringe Managua, to which the tourists and the seminarians used to go (their eyes averted from the slums) to view the Footprints. One of these seminarians, the poet Leonel Rugama, became a Sandinista, and in the sections of the poem which are addressed to him Cardenal expresses their shared view of "Revolution" as the natural next stage of "Evolution"—a process started in the stars, millions of years ago, and which will require social metamorphoses as startling as those from caterpillar into chrysalis or chrysalis to butterfly. Rugama was cornered in a house in Managua by the National Guard on January 15, 1970, along with two other young urban guerrillas, and the siege of the house where they holed up was watched by thousands of Managuans—as helicopters, planes, and even tanks were brought in to eliminate them. This small but epic incident in the Sandinista saga is made to interact, at numerous levels and in various complex ways, with the far greater catastrophe of the earthquake, in a highly intricate poetic structure.

After "Oracle over Managua," the "Trip to New York" (*"Viaje a Nueva York"*) seems easy, and neither "Epistle" poses such problems of interpretation as the earlier poems because Cardenal's attitudes are stated more explicitly, for patently didactic purposes, while "Lights" (*"Luces"*) is equally accessible. The visual and associative material used to frame the ideas in these four poems is, however, handled with Cardenal's accustomed skill: shifts of focus or of angle; cuts from close up or detail shots right through to extreme long; jump-cuts for the sake of concision and abruptness; the poetic equivalent of pans and zooms; deft insert shots (to give additional data); the use of flashbacks (and flash-forwards), or of bridging shots (like those of railway wheels or newspapers in films); foreshortening and forelengthening, applied both to space and to time (where films would use the time lapse camera or slow motion); studied relational editing; match-cuts which link two disparate scenes by the repetition of an action or a shape (or a sound)—but most of all the dialectical process of "collisional" montage, which generates fresh meaning out of the meanings of adjacent shots. Cardenal's highly visual poetry displays the verbal equivalent of each of those effects, and many of his most vivid sequences could almost serve as detailed shooting scripts.

All these devices, together with Poundian textual collage and the full range of more traditional poetic or rhetorical effects, are used in the course of Cardenal's documentary "redemption of reality," which successively "corroborates," "debunks," or "mediates" things, people, and events in a validation process designed to govern what we are to consider "true" and "real" and "meritorious" (or "false"— "illusory"—"contemptible") when viewed from the standpoint of his brave new revolutionary world.

He obliges us to interact with the physical and social world, sheds moral light on it, involves us inescapably in its affairs, and then requires us to judge what he displays—clearly expecting us to share his verdicts (be they stated or implied) and hoping we may follow his revolutionary example. In the Latin American context, which is where his documentary poems are most obviously "relevant," many people are doing just that, and the ideas which he communicates (whether obliquely or directly) are clearly around to stay and must be reckoned with:

> They've told me I talk only about politics now.
> It's not about politics but about Revolution
> which for me is the same thing as the kingdom of God.

> ("Epistle to José Coronel Urtecho")

Saint Catherine's College, Oxford   Robert Pring-Mill

NOTES

[1] James Monaco, *How to Read a Film,* (New York: Oxford University Press, 1977), p. 307.

[2] By Ronald Christ, in *Commonweal,* 100:8 (1974), pp. 89–91.

[3] Translated by Monique and Carlos Altschul (Baltimore: The Johns Hopkins University Press, 1973).

[4] *El evangelio en Solentiname,* 2 vols. (Salamanca: Ediciones Sígueme, 1976 and 1977). Donald D. Walsh's English version is published by Orbis Books, Maryknoll, New York.

[5] *La santidad de la revolución* (Salamanca: Ediciones Sígueme, 1976).

[6] See "Conversation Between Brothers" (in *Movement,* No. 35, 1978, pp. 3–4), in which Cardenal's "Open Letter" is followed by one from Daniel Berrigan to Cardenal called "Guns Don't Work" (reprinted from the *National Catholic Reporter*).

PAUL W. BORGESON, JR., received his Ph.D. from Vanderbilt University and since 1977 has been an assistant professor of Spanish at the University of North Carolina at Chapel Hill. He has published articles and papers on Ernesto Cardenal, Nicanor Parra, Juan Rulfo, and Gabriel García Marquez. His book *Hacia el hombre nuevo: poesía and pensamiento de Ernesto Cardenal* will soon be brought out by the Universidad Nacional Autónoma de México.

JONATHAN COHEN, poet and translator, worked on the translation of Enrique Lihn's *The Dark Room and Other Poems* (New Directions, 1978). Now teaching in the English Department of the State University of New York at Stony Brook, he is the author of *Poems from the Island* (Street Press, 1979) and the founding director of the Islands and Continents Translation Award.

ROBERT PRING-MILL has taught Spanish literature since 1952 at the University of Oxford, where he has held the Spanish Fellowship at St. Catherine's College since 1965. His numerous publications concern Spanish Golden Age prose fiction and drama, medieval thought and science, and twentieth-century committed poetry.

The late DONALD D. WALSH was graduated from Harvard magna cum laude in 1925 and subsequently taught Spanish and French at Exeter, Canterbury, Choate, and the Hammonasset School. Among his various activities, he was from 1953 to 1955, and again from 1959 to 1965, the director of the Modern Language Association's Foreign Language Program. He made a number of translations from the Spanish, most notably of works by Pablo Neruda and Ernesto Cardenal, and received the Chicago Review Translation Award in 1976. He was putting the finishing touches to the present volume at the time of his death in mid-1980.

ZERO HOUR

Tropical nights in Central America,
with moonlit lagoons and volcanoes
and lights from presidential palaces,
barracks and sad curfew warnings.
"Often while smoking a cigarette
I've decided that a man should die,"
says Ubico smoking a cigarette . . .
In his pink-wedding-cake palace
Ubico has a head cold. Outside, the people
were dispersed with phosphorous bombs.
San Salvador laden with night and espionage,
with whispers in homes and boardinghouses
and screams in police stations.
Carías' palace stoned by the people.
A window of his office has been smashed,
and the police have fired upon the people.
And Managua the target of machine guns
from the chocolate-cookie palace
and steel helmets patrolling the streets.

Watchman! What hour is it of the night?
Watchman! What hour is it of the night?

The *campesinos* of Honduras used to carry their money in their hats
when the *campesinos* sowed their seed
and the Hondurans were masters of their land.
When there was money
and there were no foreign loans
or taxes for J. P. Morgan & Co.,
and the fruit company wasn't competing with the little dirt farmer.
But the United Fruit Company arrived
with its subsidiaries the Tela Railroad Company
and the Trujillo Railroad Company
allied with the Cuyamel Fruit Company

and Vaccaro Brothers & Company
later Standard Fruit & Steamship Company
of the Standard Fruit & Steamship Corporation:
                    the United Fruit Company
with its revolutions for the acquisition of concessions
and exemptions of millions in import duties
and export duties, revisions of old concessions
and grants for new exploitations,
violations of contracts, violations
of the Constitution . . .
And all the conditions are dictated by the Company
with liabilities in case of confiscation
(liabilities of the nation, not of the Company)
and the conditions imposed by the latter (the Company)
for the return of the plantations to the nation
(given free by the nation to the Company)
at the end of 99 years . . .
"and all the other plantations belonging
to any other person or companies or enterprises
which may be dependents of the contractors and in which
this latter has or may have in the future
any interest of any kind will be as a consequence
included in the previous terms and conditions . . ."
(Because the Company also corrupted prose.)
The condition was that the Company build the Railroad,
but the Company wasn't building it,
because in Honduras mules were cheaper than the Railroad,
and "a Gongressman was chipper than a mule,"
                    as Zemurray used to say,
even though he continued to enjoy tax exemptions
and a grant of 175,000 acres for the Company,
with the obligation to pay the nation for each mile
that he didn't build, but he didn't pay anything to the nation
even though he didn't build a single mile (Carías is the dictator
who didn't build the greatest number of miles of railroad)
and after all, that shitty railroad was
of no use at all to the nation
because it was a railroad between two plantations
and not between the cities of Trujillo and Tegucigalpa.

They corrupt the prose and they corrupt the Congress.
The banana is left to rot on the plantations,
or to rot in the cars along the railroad tracks
or it's cut overripe so it can be rejected

when it reaches the wharf or be thrown into the sea;
the bunches of bananas declared bruised, or too skinny,
or withered, or green, or overripe, or diseased:
so there'll be no cheap bananas,
                    or so as to buy bananas cheap.
Until there's hunger along the Atlantic Coast of Nicaragua.

And the farmers are put in jail for not selling at 30 cents
and their bananas are slashed with bayonets
and the Mexican Trader Steamship sinks their barges on them
and the strikers are cowed with bullets.
(And the Nicaraguan congressmen are invited to a garden party.)
But the black worker has seven children.
And what can you do? You've got to eat,
And you've got to accept what they offer to pay.
                    24 cents a bunch.
While the Tropical Radio Subsidiary was cabling Boston:
"We assume that Boston will give its approval to
the payment made to the Nicaraguan congressmen of the majority
        party
because of the incalculable benefits that it represents for
        the Company."
And from Boston to Galveston by telegraph
and from Galveston by cable and telegraph to Mexico
and from Mexico by cable to San Juan del Sur
and from San Juan del Sur by telegraph to Puerto Limón
and from Puerto Limón by canoe way into the mountains
arrives the order of the United Fruit Company:
"United is buying no more bananas."
And workers are laid off in Puerto Limón.
And the little workshops close.
Nobody can pay his debts.
And the bananas rotting in the railroad cars.
                    So there'll be no cheap bananas
                    And so that there'll be bananas cheap,
                        19 cents a bunch.
The workers get IOUs instead of wages.
Instead of payment, debts,
And the plantations are abandoned, for they're useless now,
and given to colonies of unemployed.
And the United Fruit Company in Costa Rica
with its subsidiaries the Costa Rica Banana Company
and the Northern Railway Company and

the International Radio Telegraph Company
and the Costa Rica Supply Company
                are fighting in court against an orphan.
The cost of a derailment is $25 in damages
(but it would have cost more to repair the track).

And congressmen, cheaper than mules, Zemurray used to say.
Sam Zemurray, the Turkish banana peddler
in Mobile, Alabama, who one day took a trip to New Orleans
and on the wharves saw United throwing bananas into the sea
and he offered to buy all the fruit to make vinegar,
he bought it, and he sold it right there in New Orleans
and United had to give him land in Honduras
to get him to break his contract in New Orleans,
and that's how Sam Zemurray abbointed bresidents in Jonduras.
He provoked border disputes between Guatemala and Honduras
(which meant between the United Fruit Company and *his* company)
proclaiming that Honduras (*his* company) must not lose
"one inch of land not only in the disputed strip
but also in any other zone of Honduras
(of his company) not in dispute . . ."
(while United was defending the rights of Honduras
in its lawsuit with Nicaragua Lumber Company)
until the suit ended because he merged with United
and afterward he sold all his shares to United
and with the proceeds of the sale he bought shares in United
and with the shares he captured the presidency of Boston
(together with its employees the various presidents of Honduras)
and he was now the owner of both Honduras and Guatemala
and that was the end of the lawsuit over the exhausted lands
that were now of no use either to Guatemala or Honduras.

There was a Nicaraguan abroad,
a "Nica" from Niquinohomo,
working for the Huasteca Petroleum Co. of Tampico,
And he had five thousand dollars saved up.
And he wasn't a soldier or a politician.
And he took three thousand of the five thousand dollars
and went off to Nicaragua to join Moncada's revolution.
But by the time he arrived, Moncada was laying down his arms.
He spent three days miserable in the Peoples Hill.
Miserable, not knowing what to do.

4

And he wasn't a politician or a soldier.
He thought and thought and he finally said to himself:
"Somebody's got to do it."
                    And then he issued his first proclamation.

General Moncada sends a wire to the Americans:
ALL MY MEN AGREE TO SURRENDER EXCEPT ONE.
Mr. Stimson sends him an ultimatum.
"The people thanks you for nothing . . ."
                    is Moncada's message to the hold-out.
He assembles his men in El Chipote:
29 men (and with him, 30) against the U.S.A.
        EXCEPT ONE.
                        ("One from Niquinohomo . . .")
And with him, 30!
"Anyone who sets out to be a savior winds up on the Cross,"
says Moncada in another message.
Because Moncada and Sandino were neighbors;
Moncada from Masatepe and Sandino from Niquinohomo.
And Sandino replies to Moncada:
"Death is quite unimportant."
And to Stimson: "I have faith in the courage of my men . . ."
And to Stimson, after the first defeat:
"Anybody that thinks we're defeated
                    doesn't know my men."
And he wasn't a soldier or a politician.
And his men:
                    many of them were kids,
with palm-leaf hats and sandals
or barefoot, with machetes, old men
with white beards, twelve-year-olds with their rifles,
whites, inscrutable Indians, and blonds, and kinky-haired blacks
with tattered pants and with no provisions,
their pants in shreds,
parading in Indian file with the flag up front—
a rag hoisted on a branch from the woods—
silent beneath the rain, and weary,
their sandals sloshing in the puddles of the town
                                    Long live Sandino!
and they came down from the mountain and they went back up to
        the mountain,
marching, sloshing, with the flag up front.
A barefoot or sandaled army with almost no weapons

that had neither discipline nor disorder
where neither officers nor troops got any pay
but nobody was forced to fight:
and they had different military ranks but they were all equal,
everybody getting the same food
and clothing, the same ration for everybody.
And the officers had no aides:
more like a community than an army
and more united by love than by military discipline
even though there has never been greater unity in an army.
A happy army, with guitars and hugs.
A love song was its battle hymn:

> "If Adelita went off with another guy
> I'd go after her by land and by sea.
> If by sea on an armored cruiser
> And if by land on an armored train."

"We all greet each other with hugs,"
Sandino used to say—and nobody hugged like him.
And whenever they talked about themselves they'd say "all":
"All of us . . ." "We're all equal."
"Here we're all brothers," Umanzor used to say.
And they were all united until they were all killed.
Fighting against airplanes with hayseed troops,
with no pay except food and clothing and arms,
and hoarding each bullet as though it were made of gold;
with mortars made out of pipes
and with bombs made out of rocks and pieces of glass,
stuffed with dynamite from the mines and wrapped in hides;
with hand grenades made of sardine cans.

"He's a *bandido*," Somoza used a say, "a *bandolero*."
And Sandino never owned any property.
Which, translated, means:
it was Somoza calling Sandino an outlaw.
And Sandino never owned any property.
And at banquets Moncada called him a bandit
and up in the mountains Sandino had no salt
and his men shivering with cold in the mountains,
and he mortgaged his father-in-law's house
in order to free Nicaragua, while in the Presidential Mansion
Moncada had Nicaragua mortgaged.

6

"Of course he isn't one," said the American Minister
laughing, "but we call him a bandit technically."

What's that light way off there? Is it a star?
It's Sandino's light shining in the black mountain.
There they are, he and his men, beside the red bonfire
with rifles slung and wrapped in their blankets,
smoking or singing sad songs from the North,
the men motionless and their shadows in motion.

His face was as vague as that of a ghost,
remote because of his brooding and thinking
and serious because of the campaigns and the wind and the rain.
And Sandino had the face not of a soldier
but of a poet changed into a soldier through necessity,
and of a nervous man controlled by serenity.
There were two faces superposed on his face:
a countenance somber and yet radiant;
sad as a mountain evening
and joyful as a mountain morning.
In the light his face became young again,
and in the shadow it filled with weariness.
And Sandino wasn't intelligent or cultured.
But he turned out to have mountain intelligence.
"In the mountain everything is a teacher," Sandino used to say
(dreaming of Segovias filled with schools)
and he got messages from all the mountains
and it seemed as if every cabin was spying for him
(where foreigners were like brothers,
all foreigners, even the Americans)
          "even the Yankees . . .
And: "God will speak through the Segovians . . ." he would say.
"I never thought I'd come out of this war alive
but I've always believed it was a necessary war . . ."
And: "Do they think I'm going to turn into a big landowner?"

It's midnight in the Segovia Mountains.
And that light is Sandino! A light with a song . . .

          "If Adelita went off with another guy."

But nations have their destiny.
And Sandino never became president.
It was Sandino's murderer who became president
and he was president for 20 years!

7

"If Adelita went off with another guy
I'd go after her by land and by sea."

The truce was signed. They loaded the arms onto wagons.
Blunderbusses held together with hemp rope, scaly rifles
and a few old machine guns.
And the wagons came down through the mountains.

"If by sea on an armored cruiser
And if by land on an armored train."

A telegram from the American Minister (Mr. Lane)
to the Secretary of State, sent in Managua
on the 14th of February 1934 at 6:05 p.m.
and received in Washington at 8:50 p.m.
"Informed by official sources
that the plane could not land in Wiwilí
and that Sandino's arrival is therefore delayed . . ."

The telegram of the American Minister (Mr. Lane)
to the Secretary of State on the 16th of February
announcing Sandino's arrival in Managua
Not Printed
was not printed in the State Dept. memorandum.

Like the otter that came out of the thicket
onto the highway and is surrounded by dogs
and stands still facing the hunters
because it knows it has nowhere to go . . .

"I talked with Sandino for half an hour,"
said Somoza to the American Minister,
"but I can't tell you what he talked about
because I don't know what he talked about,
because I don't know what he talked about."

"And so, you see, I'll never own any property" . . .
And "It is un-con-sti-tu-tion-al," Sandino would say.
"The National Guard is unconstitutional."
"An insult!" said Somoza to the American Minister
on the twenty-first of February at 6:00 p.m.
"An insult! I want to stop Sandino."

8

Four prisoners are digging a hole.
"Who's dead?" asked one prisoner.
"Nobody," said the guard.
"Then what's the hole for?"
"None of your business," said the guard, "Go on digging."

The American Minister is having lunch with Moncada.
"Will you have coffee, sir?"
Moncada sits looking out the window.
"Will you have coffee, sir?
It's very good coffee, sir."
"What?" Moncada looks away from the window
toward the servant: "Oh, yes, I'll have coffee."
And he laughed, "Certainly."

In a barracks five men are in a locked room
with guards at the doors and windows.
One of the men has only one arm.
The fat bemedaled officer comes in and he says to them: "Yes."

Another man is going to have supper with the President that night
(the man for whom they were digging the hole)
and he tells his friends: "Let's go. It's time."
And they go up to have supper with the President of Nicaragua.

At 10:00 p.m. they drive down to Managua.
Halfway down the guards stop them.
The two oldest are taken off in one car
and the other three in another car in another direction,
to where four prisoners had been digging a hole.
"Where are we going?"
asked the man they made the hole for.
            And nobody answered him.

Then the car stopped and a guard said to them:
"Get out." The three of them got out,
and a one-armed man shouted: "Fire!"

"I was at a concert," said Somoza.
And it was true, he had been at a concert

or at a banquet or watching a dancer dance or
at some crap or other.
And at 10 o'clock that night Somoza was scared.
Suddenly out there the phone rang.
"Sandino is on the phone!"
And he was scared. One of his friends said:
"Don't be an idiot, you goddamned fool!"
Somoza said not to answer the phone.
The dancer went on dancing for the murderer.
And out there in the dark the phone went on
                    ringing and ringing.

By the light of a flood lamp
four guards are filling in a hole.
And by the light of a February moon.

It's the hour when the corn-mush star of Chontales
gets the little Indian girls up to make corn mush,
and out come the chicle-seller, the wood-seller, and the root-seller,
with the banana groves still silvered by the moon,
with the cry of the coyote and the honey bear
and the hooting of the owl in the moonlight.
The pacas and the agoutis come out of their holes
and the tickbirds and the *cadejos* hide in theirs.
The Weeper goes weeping along the river banks:
"D'you find him?" "No!" "D'you find him?" "No!"
A bird cackles like the creaking of a tree,
then the ravine is hushed as if listening to something,
and suddenly a scream . . . The bird utters
the same sad word, the same sad word.
The ranch hands begin to herd their cows:
Tooo-to-to-to; Tooo-to-to-to; Tooo-to-to-to;
the boatmen hoist the sails of their boats;
the telegraph clerk in San Rafael del Norte wires:
GOOD MORNING ALL IS WELL IN SAN RAFAEL DEL
    NORTE
and the telegraph clerk in Juigalpa: ALL IS WELL IN JUIGALPA.
And the Tuca squaws keep coming down the Hidden River
with the ducks going quack-quack-quack, and the echoes,
the echoes, while the tugboat goes with the Tuca squaws
slithering over the green-glass river
toward the Atlantic . . .

And meanwhile in the drawing rooms of the Presidential Mansion
and in the prison yards and in the barracks
and in the American Legation and in the Police Station
those who kept watch that night saw one another in the ghostly dawn
with hands and faces as though stained with blood.

"I did it," Somoza said afterward.
"I did it, for the good of Nicaragua."

And William Walker said, when they were going to execute him:
"The President of Nicaragua is a Nicaraguan."

In April, in Nicaragua, the fields are dry.
It's the month of brush burning,
of heat, and pastures covered with embers,
and coal-colored hills;
of hot winds, and air that smells charred,
and of fields made blue by the smoke
and the dust clouds of the tractors uprooting trees;
of the riverbeds dry as roads
and the branches stripped like roots;
of suns blurred and blood-red
and moons huge and red as suns
and the far-off brush fires, at night, like stars.

In May come the first rains.
The tender grass is reborn from the ashes.
The muddy tractors plough the earth.
The roads fill with butterflies and puddles,
and the nights are cool, and insect-laden,
and it rains all night. In May
the *malinches* blossom in the streets of Managua.
But April in Nicaragua is the month of death.
They killed them in April.
I was with them in the April rebellion
and I learned to handle a Rising machine gun.
            And Adolfo Báez Bone was my friend:
They hunted him with airplanes, with trucks,
with floodlights, with tear-gas bombs,

with radios, with dogs, with police;
and I remember the red clouds over the Presidential Mansion
like blood-red swabs of cotton,
and the red moon over the Presidential Mansion.
The underground radio kept saying he was alive.
The people didn't believe he had died.
                    (And he hasn't died.)

Because at times a man is born in a land
                    and he *is* that land.
And the land in which that man is buried
                    is that man.
And the men who afterward are born in that land
                    are that man.
And Adolfo Báez Bone was that man.

"If they asked me to choose my fate"
(Báez Bone had said to me three days before)
"to choose between dying murdered like Sandino
or being President like Sandino's murderer
I'd choose Sandino's fate."
                    And he did choose his fate.
Glory isn't what the history books teach:
it's a flock of buzzards in a field and a great stink.

            But when a hero dies
                    he doesn't die:
            for that hero is reborn
                    in a Nation.

Afterward the U.S.A. sent more arms to Somoza;
it took about half a morning for the arms to go by;
trucks and trucks loaded with crates of arms
all marked U.S.A. MADE IN U.S.A.,
arms to catch more prisoners, to hunt down books,
to steal five pesos from Juan Potosme.
I saw those arms going along Roosevelt Avenue.
And people silent in the streets watched them go by:
the skinny one, the barefoot one, the one with the bicycle,
the black one, the blubber-lipped, the girl dressed in yellow,
the tall one, the blond, the bald one, the one with the big mustache,
the snub-nosed one, the straight-haired, the kinky-haired,
        the squat one,

and the faces of all those people
                     were the face of a dead ex-lieutenant.

The mambo music used to come down as far as Managua.
With his eyes red and blurred like the eyes of a shark
but a shark with a bodyguard and armaments
(*Nicaraguan shark*)
Somoza was dancing the mambo
                              mambo mambo
                              yummy mambo
when they were killing them.
And Tachito Somoza (the son) goes up to the Presidential Mansion
to change a blood-stained shirt
for a clean one.
                     Stained with blood and chili.
The prison dogs would howl with pity.
People living near the barracks would hear the screams.
At first it was a single scream in the middle of the night,
and afterward more and more screams
and afterward a silence . . . Then a volley
and a single shot. Afterward another silence,
                              and an ambulance.

And in the jail the dogs are howling again!
The sound of the iron door closing
behind you and then the questions begin
and the accusation, the accusation of conspiracy
and the confession, and then the hallucinations,
the snapshot of your wife shining like a spotlight
in front of you and the nights filled with shrieks
and with noises and with silence, a tomblike silence,
and again the same question, the same question,
and the same noise repeated and the spotlight in your eyes
and then the long months that followed.
Oh, to be able to sleep in your own bed tonight
without the fear of being pulled out of bed and taken out of
         your house,
the fear of knocks on the door or doorbells ringing in the night!

Shots sound in the night, or they seem to be shots.
Heavy trucks go by, and they stop,
and they go on. You've heard their voices.

It's at the corner. They must be changing the guard.
You've heard their laughter and their weapons.
The tailor across the street has turned on his light.
And it seemed as though they knocked here. Or at the tailor's.
Maybe tonight you're on the list!
And the night goes on. And there's a lot of night left.
And the day will be only a sunlit night.
The quietness of night under the scorching sun.

Mr. Whelan, the American Minister,
attends the party at the Presidential Mansion.
The lights of the Mansion can be seen all over Managua.
The music from the party reaches even the prison cells
in the gentle breeze of Managua under Martial Law.
The prisoners in their cells manage to hear the music
among the screams of prisoners getting electric shocks.
Up at the Mansion Mr. Whelan says:
                                                      "Fine party!"

As the sonofabitch Roosevelt said to Sumner Welles:
"Somoza is a sonofabitch
                              but he's ours."

A slave to foreigners
                    and a tyrant to his people
imposed by intervention
                    and kept in power by nonintervention
SOMOZA FOREVER

The spy who goes out by day
The agent who goes out by night
and the night arrest:
Those who are jailed for talking on a bus
or for shouting Hurray
or for a joke.
"Accused of talking against His Excellency the President . . ."
And the ones judged by a toad-faced judge
or in Courts Martial with dog-faced guards;
and the ones forced to drink piss and eat shit
(when you all get a Constitution, remember them)
the ones with the bayonet in the mouth and the needle in the eye,
the electric shocks and the spotlight in the eyes.
"He's a sonofabitch, Mr. Welles, but he's *ours*."

And in Guatemala, in Costa Rica, in Mexico,
the exiles wake up at night screaming,
dreaming that they're getting the "little machine" again,
or that they're tied up once more
watching Tachito coming at them with the needle.
". . . And he was good-looking, you know . . .

                                        (said a *campesino*).
"Yes, it was him. And good-looking, you know . . .
White skin, with his little yellow
short-sleeved shirt.
                    The good-looking bastard."

When night falls in Nicaragua the Presidential Mansion
fills with shadows. And faces appear.
Faces in the darkness.
                    Blood-covered faces.
Adolfo Báez Bone; Pablo Leal without a tongue;
my classmate Luis Gabuardi whom they burned alive
and he died shouting *Death to Somoza!*
The face of the sixteen-year-old telegraph clerk
(we don't even know his name)
who sent secret messages at night
to Costa Rica, trembling telegrams across
the night, from the dark Nicaragua of Tacho
(and the boy won't be mentioned in the history books)
and he was caught, and he died looking at Tachito;
his face is still looking at him. The kid
they caught at night sticking up posters
                    SOMOZA IS A THIEF
and some laughing guards drag him off into the woods . . .
And so many other shadows, so many other shadows;
the shadows of the flocks of buzzards at Wilwilí;
the shadow of Estrada; the shadow of Umanzor;
the shadow of Socrates Sandino;
and the great shadow, the one of the great crime,
the shadow of Augusto César Sandino.
Every night in Managua the Presidential Mansion
fills with shadows.

But the hero is born when he dies
and green grass is reborn from the ashes.

1956   [D. D. W.]

NICARAGUAN CANTO

To the FSLN

During May the thrush sings in the morning
             when the rains are starting,
but toward evening in July, when the day's showers are over,
             the thrush sings sweetly and
in freedom, in the North. Later, the
trumpeting *zanate, Cassidix nicaragüensis*
(a Nicaraguan bird) flies blueblackviolet
in October, or November, over Nicaraguan villages.
It is a proletarian bird: no glamor, always
found among the poor.
The "throat-cut-bird" (red splash on neck)
             sings in the orchards.
The *toledo,* black velvet with a scarlet cap,
             sings TO-LE-DO TO-LE-DO where coffee grows.
The *pijul,* night-colored in its plumage, sings
             PEA-HOOL PEA-HOOL PEA-HOOL
             (and eats the ticks off cattle).
The beggar-bird calls out
             TRES-PESOS TRES-PESOS TRES-PESOS.
The lesser oriole sings in the fields its tail tip-tilted
and every moonlit night the owl laments in cemeteries and ruins.
The "shrieker" of the River Escondido: always hidden
             one hears the shriek one never sees the bird.
             In the hills of Curinguás there are *quetzales.* . . .
In summer iguanas lay their eggs.
             Lizards are born in early winter.
Frogs begin to croak with the first rains in May.
             In June the thrush constructs its nest.
The alligators which have phosphorescent eyes at night
             lay their eggs in July
when turtles bury theirs along the beach
on moonless nights. Then come the storms. It is

the season of gales. Those heavy joyful downpours.
Called the "Just Judge" (from its song) the *justo juez*
                    sings JUSTO-JUEZ JUSTO-JUEZ JUSTO-JUEZ
            all through September on the barbed-wire fences.
                    And in September migrant swallows crowd the lake.
October: the fork-tail ducks arrive the swallows leave
assembling first on telegraph wires along the roads.
            Crows pass through Matagalpa in November
and they return in May when the corn is young
                    to eat its tender cobs, a *campesino* said.
In December the odor of insecticide is in the air
        and in December the *zanates* lay their eggs
                    (their young hatch out in March, and there's
a clamor in their nests all summer up
        the palm trees).
In January the golden orioles begin to build:
neat golden nests suspended from *pijivay* palms;
                    they lay in February, and by
                            October their deserted nests are like
a village of thatched huts abandoned
to slow disintegration by the wind.
                    In February cedars flower
and the *buenos-días* sings on the Atlantic coast while nest building.
Oak trees in Solentiname bloom in March above the lake with
                    blossoms rosy as girls' lips.
And in summer: the *chichitote* sings the loveliest
                    song of any bird in Nicaragua
and the *cucurruchí* sings its name in summer nest building
while the shellfish are harvested in Bluefields Bay—
                    in March and April—and
in Ocotal, in April, the *quetzal* rears its young.

But another country found it needed all these riches.
To obtain the 1911 loans Nicaragua had to cede her customs rights
also the running of the National Bank
to lenders who reserved the right
to take it over. For those of 1912
she pledged the railroads also. On Feb. 2, 1911,
the banking group Brown Brothers & Co. acquired
an interest in us. Paying off one loan
            meant setting up another, and
so on. (Once in there's no way out.)

Bankers gathered round like barracudas.
The Marines landed "to re-establish order"
and they stayed in Nicaragua for 13 years. Control
over railroads customs banks was not enough.
        Nicaragua sold her territory as well
On 35 dollars a week Adolfo Díaz,
an Angeles Mining Co. employee, became the "capitalist"
of the "revolution" lending 600,000 dollars to the "cause."
The repayment of the Brown Brothers loan
        was underwritten with the customs revenue.
Corruption, national corruption was the bankers' banquet
        a buzzards' banquet
a ring of buzzard-gentlemen in morning coats.
Politicians: like blind bats hanging over us
        to shit upon us in the dark and piss on us
the shit and piss of bats as black as night
        black wings beating black air.
500,000 dollars more borrowed to stabilize the exchange
but—oh the bankers' banquet—
nor does the money even have to leave New York.
        The pledge involved placing the country in the bankers' hands.
The loan of 1911 was negotiated to establish
a National Bank which never left the foreign bankers' hands.
Brown Brothers went and bought what "paper" they desired
(I mean what paper money they desired) at 20 pesos to the dollar
while selling at 12.50, what paper they desired
which means that 20 pesos cost a single dollar (and they could
buy up as many as they wished) but when sold back
(which they could do at will) were worth one dollar sixty. I.e.
        they bought their money cheap to sell it dear
bought it from Nicaragua to sell it back
which pushed our prices up: corn, housing, education,
dances, railroad tickets.
        That was how the banker-mafia's looting worked.
        They attacked our national currency like gangsters.
And then the bankers lent the land its money back
at 6%.
The national revenues: collected by those foreign bankers
placed in a National Bank controlled by the same
foreign bankers, and distributed by the same foreign
bankers in association with the U.S. Secretary of State
(himself a shareholder of the Angeles Mining Co.).

18

Like the Honduran taxes taken up by Morgan
Morgan the fierce
            like the wild boar's slashing charge
                or the stench of puma on the wind.
Later even national territory was sold (under
the Bryan-Chamorro Treaty) for 3 million dollars
which also went straight into the foreign bankers' hands.
(Whereby the United States acquired exclusive rights
                over a Canal Zone 2 Caribbean isles
                one naval base
our country for 3 million dollars—the cash to the bankers—
the customs continuing in the lenders' hands for
an unspecified period—till all debts should be paid—
and the lenders have acquired the National Bank, likewise
the State Railroad where they bought a 51% interest for
1 million dollars more, until of all that once
made up the nation only the flag remained.)
            Dark night. The hut without kerosene.
            An owl hoots mournfully over the land.
The little *pijul's* song is silenced.
There was no need for actual annexation financial
domination satisfied the States (with power over all presidents
from Díaz to the present incumbent) giving
all the advantages of annexation without the risks or the expense.
"Unless one simply plays with words"—a professor,
to the *Daily News*, in Paris, *ca.* 1928—
"nobody doubts that Nicaragua's independence
            is nonexistent."
To invest capital in Nicaragua and then protect
U.S. investments was the State Department's job.
Political expansion with a view to economic expansion:
economic expansion because capital did not produce enough
in the United States or not as much
as it could do in Nicaragua
THAT IS: imperialism namely
                interventions for investments or vice versa.
Diplomacy held the country in subjection through the bankers
and the bankers got the money out of Nicaragua by diplomacy.
            The mourning buzzards gathered round in morning dress.
Round Nicaragua's G.N.P.—
        just as sharks when they scent blood.
Internal disorganization and corruption fostered foreign

intervention consequently intervention fostered the
disorganization and corruption and developed them
       (that stares you in the face).
Whence, therefore:
imperialism as a disturbing and disrupting element etc.
fostering backwardness corruption etc. in Nicaragua: violating
treaties constitutions judicial decisions
       provoking civil war manipulating elections bribing
it has protected thieves prostituted politics impoverished the people
impeded union kept its agents in power against the people's will:
       thereby raised the cost of living defended
              oppression and brought death.
Thus Nicaragua (when Sandino appeared) found herself with
part of her territory alienated, the external debt
sky high, financial life entirely subject to
the group of New York bankers, and no progress.
              The whole country
as Cape Thanks Be to God is now: down to a single
line of huts, one street, and in it, six feet from the sea,
a buzzard squabbling over fish guts with a dog.

I said iguanas lay their eggs . . . It is the process. They
(or else the frogs) in the silence of the carboniferous age
              made the first sound
       sang the first love song here on earth
       sang the first love song here beneath the moon
              it is the process.
The process started with the stars.
              New relations of production: that too
is part of the process. Oppression. After oppression, liberation.
The Revolution started in the stars, millions
       of light-years away. The egg of life
       is one. From
the first bubble of gas, to the iguana's egg, to the New Man.
Sandino was proud he had been born "from the womb of the
       oppressed"
              (that of an Indian girl from Niquinohomo).
From the womb of the oppressed the Revolution will be born.
It is the process.
The male pelican puffs out his chest to court the female
              before mating.

But the process still goes further:
Che smiling beyond death as though just back from Hades.

"Mahomet's Paradise" about which Gage spoke
    I tell you Paradise has been sold up.
The Promised Land divided by *latifundistas!*
    The land where I belong, just like
the *tigüilotera* dove or big-foot pigeon.
      Nindirí, Niquinohomo, Monimbó
      Nandaime, Diriá, Diriomo.
Ox of our youth which Darío once saw puffing vapor.
   The clamorous peahens which we heard when we were lads.
   The loud-mouthed swearing. We'd go to the river's mouth for clams.
   The "cactus-hopper" in the cactus hedges.
Jays squabbling over mangoes, robbing nests.
Green parakeets along a branch, like shrieking leaves;
and when they rise you'd think the branch was flying!
There was a *curré* calling on a dry pole meaning drought.
    5 p.m. and the handslap of *tortillas* being made
      and the smell of the *tortillas* on the griddle
and the scent of woodsmoke. The hour
when the washerwomen return to Nindirí from the lagoon.
    A flight of herons over Lake Managua.
The hour I'd go to meet my girl friend from the typing school . . .
    The hour when the first lights go on, and
    the last pairs of macaws fly homeward.
Managua: Rubén long-haired, with girl friend, on the quay
watching the white herons, and the brown.
    The evening breeze's soft caress.
      He with his "brown heron." The first kiss.
How often have we Nicaraguans overseas said over drinks
"ours is a land of shit"? In cheap hotels
where exiles meet, but then
we'd start remembering *tamales*, and tripe soup
    with coriander and wild chili peppers, the songs
to the Purísima in December (with the scent of *madroño* trees
  in bloom)
      the blue-blue lake and on the lake the flight
      of a heron like a white-white sail
     or the small sailing boat that's like a heron
and one began to think about
the scents of May: the warmth and smell of Nicaragua

a rainy patio and the roof tiles wet
    tic tic tic tic tic tic tic tic
the small sound of water dripping off the roof
the whistle of the steamship *Victoria* as it draws near Granada
    a land—we said—deserving better luck.
And one has also thought about:
        windmills looking in the distance like iron roses,
        the song a railway engine sings in open country,
bringing the cattle home, milking early in the morning,
the smell of cheese in the cheese-women's boats
    a line of telegraph poles slanting across a meadow . . .
The *Victoria* at the quayside, or a TACA plane.
    A cottonfield in flower, looking like snow,
        a tractor working in it
            with the shape of Momotombo in the
            background.
And the little diesel train to León which hugs the lake.
Or:
        Momotombo lit by the setting sun
          the lake all orange-yellow like the scales of a *mojarra*
    a youngster fishing in Mateare
            and the whistle of that León train.
Rubén always made the trip from Momotombo to Managua
in a little steamer. Watching the white herons,
and the brown. The lovely women. Sipping their cocktails
or cognac, he tells us, in the small saloon.
        Flowers provoked in him a feeling of voluptuous lassitude.
On a coffee plantation, a girl the color of chocolate
gave him clear water in a gourd. He saw the gourd was carved
        with shields, birds, letters, floral patterns, geometrical
        designs.
Masaya made him think of Hafiz: flowers in the gardens, flowers
in women's hair; the mayor had had the main street strewn with
    flowers.
Volcán Masaya: standing close to Nindirí. (In ages past, so
    Victor Hugo says,
Momotombo did not love Masaya's god because he was
so cruel.) Oh don't hit me . . . Oh don't hit me . . .
Ay mamita! Or you'll kill me . . . *Ay mamita!* His face
one livid mass. Nosecheeksforehead all one livid mass. The left eye
almost out. And the Major: Hit him harder . . . Hit him
    harder . . .

Kill him! Beating with the butt of his own carbine, bellowing:
Hit him harder! Harder! Harder! Kill the bastard! Kill . . .
He's got to die. The soldiers kept on beating
him with bundles of electric wires. He lay there naked
in the water trough. Hit him! Hit him harder! Go on hitting . . .
Kill . . . Kill . . . And then he took the wires himself.
And started kicking him. Right on the heart. You bastard, I'll
soon kill you (and the Major wound a steel wire round his neck).
The lad ran fifteen yards and fell. Left eye half out.
The right side of his face so swollen that it seemed to join
the neck. Dragged himself as far as the latrine. And died.
The body was thrown down the crater of Volcán Masaya:
the "Hell" of Masaya, as the Spaniards called it. Oviedo,
who had seen it: "In the deepest and the furthest part
of this great pit there was a liquid fire, of the consistency
of water, brighter than redhot coals; more fiery
than fire itself, if the expression be permitted;
and boiling, not everywhere but here and there,
the seething wandering from place to place,
with a continuous plopping bubbling sound from end to end.
According to the Indian headman Nindirí, at certain times
a naked wizened hag would rise out of the pit to tell
them whether they were going to win, or else that it was going to rain
and there would be much corn; and they threw in a man
as sacrifice: or perhaps two, or more,
some women maybe, and some boys and girls. But
since the Christians came that wizened hag
rose much less often. Indeed hardly ever. Saying Christians were
all evil and till they were gone she would not meet the Indians.
He added she was very old and wrinkled, breasts down
to her bellybutton; hair scanty and swept back; teeth long and sharp,
like those of dogs; skin far darker than the Indians';
eyes sunken, blazing . . ."
          For the Devil "was a murderer from the beginning."

Then there was Don Manuel Zavala, self-exiled in New York
since 20, saying at 75 that he would not return
to Nicaragua while the Gangster stayed in power
          (never calling him by name: just "the Gangster");
when a sick man he came back to his sisters' house, the Gangster
still in power; dying in his dear Granada, under the Gangster's rule.
Coronel knew an old man in Granada who said (who often said):
"I wish I were a foreigner, so that I could go home."

Or Gilberto who dreamed of emigrating, anywhere; to England
for example, "but with the Lake of Nicaragua, *zanates*, the
Granada-to-Managua train, pig's crackling with yucca, and
        Coronel Urtecho."

                Sails and herons on the deep deep blue.
            A lake the color of blue jeans, as William put it.
Such beauty was surely given us for love.
A launch out in midlake level with San Ubaldo . . .
                moorhens over toward Colón.
            The lake by moonlight.
        The moon above the lake, the water moon-colored.
So much beauty: for equality.
                (The lake on a calm night, and a motor launch a long way
                off.)
We'd go, the gang of us, to fish for *laguneros* and *guapotes*.
". . . the land which I shall give you . . . quoth Jehovah"
            And there are old sunken wrecks
which date back to the filibusters, or the Transit Company,
Vanderbilt's old paddle-steamers in which the sharks now breed
            perhaps with just the funnel showing
among the weeds and duck droppings. (Vanderbilt didn't even know
how to say Nicaragua. He said "Nicaragay.")
            The jetty at Moyogalpa rotted through . . .
The land is not a whore
    but now they've tried to sell her to a ghost
recluse in a hotel:
                to the specter Howard Hughes.
The jetty at Moyogalpa rotted through
the black gaps which one had to jump by moonlight;
the launch which reached San Miguelito in the dawn:
they sold black coffee on the pier, and fried fish in *tortillas*
as the sun came up, with shades of green reflected in still water . . .
        A lad with a string of fish (the red and gold *mojarras*).
Land stolen from us.
Bankers, the Somoza dynasty, the Companies—they've
            stolen it, and steal it every day.
My homeland with its rivers, with my lovely rivers: huts
        with beached canoes and clothes hung out to dry
                latrines reflected in the water
and a rowing boat which heads downstream likewise reflected
cutting a sheet of glass
                    (a woman in it wearing red)

and the coffee-colored beachhen with
           lemon-yellow wings, spindle-shanked,
     deft stepping over the great water lilies
                      light as a flower itself.
The water is the hue of a *guapote*'s scales inshore
there where the yellow *sorocontil* blooms
                    a blue macaw in flight
a needle-duck swims past (snake-necked sharp-billed)
     a fast boat with an outboard motor passes
and an egret shoots out startled.
        The scent of cedar blossom.
        Hum of the sawmill by the river.
White herons at the edge each whitely mirrored.
     The new moon no broader than a slender heron.
It grows dark in the Escondido and the *cuaco* quacks.
             Here we must build a country.
We stand on the threshhold of a Promised Land
          which flows with milk and honey: like a woman
            mel et lac sub lingua tua
the kiss comes when it should and in due course the kisses
"In the land which I shall give thee keep not thy brother illiterate
that he may gather in thy cotton and thy coffee. Quoth Jehovah."
        A land promised for the Revolution.
With all things held in common
     "as they were before the Fall of our First Parents"
I have seen green banana groves
          and sugar cane a different shade of green.
A meadow of *zacate* with some cows
            and the track leading on between *ocote* pines . . .
       I've dreamed of seeing art schools here
        and nursery schools.
I recall low ridges, yellow after burning,
         then plains with calabash trees and thornbushes.
A *pocoyo* hopping along in front of the jeep at night
           its bird's eyes gleaming in the headlights. I recall
coffee plantations at Telpaneca. Tobacco growing at Jalapa.
Jícaro, where
the Coco flows over gold dust and white sand.
     Beyond Jalapa the scent of balsam firs . . .
        Or, seen from a bus:
           a windmill, a small church
           on a hill, a country cemetery.

Macaws will always fly in pairs
and cross the evening sky gossiping (or squabbling)
        in macaw language.
I recall, though I don't quite know why,
    that little shop in San Rafael del Norte, after dark,
lit up, with a group of girls inside.
I saw mountains covered in pinewoods, with mountain pigeons cooing
and the song of "little widows." There
in the square of Quilalí hangs the propeller
        of a plane Sandino's men shot down
which now serves as village bell. And there
I heard the "little widows" sing their lonely sad lament.
And there Sandino dreamed of *campesinos* running great co-operatives.
(Beyond: the huts of the Miskito Indians begin,
on stilts along the Coco River, like birds' nests.)
Houses schools transport hospitals roads adequate food
hydroelectric plants
but at present just the beauty of arriving at a palm-leaf hut
when the mosquitoes start and the first star comes out
        we saw a jaguar's paw mark and we found the hut
had been abandoned.
        And the sadness of the evening, then, and the
            mosquitoes . . .
The Tuma! Oh to see the Tuma
country once again . . . Coffee in bloom, and corn.
        In March the cobs are tender.
Mist over the coffee plantations and, in the mist,
the whitish scent of coffee flowers (like that of orange blossom)
        with *chichitotes* singing
        and the "whistler."
        Campesino campesino
        what lovely fields you have!
            it's a shame that capitalists own them.
      Or:
dark burnt fields (near San José
de los Remates) with, beyond,
forests of cedar and lignum-vitae trees—and
        toucans calling.
And a "lion bird" (long-tailed and tawny as a lion)
going POON
        POON
            POON

The forests where the *quetzal* lives which cannot live when caged;
the *quetzal*'s habitat, and that of Sandinistas.
The Bijagual: a mountain in the North, up the Musún.
The Tapacucí, the Quiabú, the Tisey, the Tomabú: all mountains
in the area of Estelí.
Pis-Pis, Condega, Yalí, Quilalí,
Yalagüina, Palacagüina
Muy-Muy
here we've dreamed of a land
for which we've fought many battles
so many battles
(Pis-Pis: Pedrón was there, he seized the mines)
and there is so much, brother, to be done . . .
Kukerawala River! Jaguars in heat roaring by moonlight
along its banks, and when they roar
the monkeys shriek in fear.
(We're going to build schools along the Kukerawala.)
A just social system
which will ensure that the rule
of social inequality does not return.
El Chipote: a damp
and misty mountain where the sun never gets through the trees,
with white-faced monkeys and macaws among the thickets: of
ocote pine
sweet gums, mahogany with creepers and lianas, that's
where "he" established his headquarters:
pocoyos screeching, jaguars roaring, toucans trilling.
High in its nest in the tallest of the liquidambar trees (at maybe
sixty feet)
the *quetzal* sings its lovely territorial song; when still,
you'd never see it, mimicking the light—
beneath a cloudy sky, its feathers are like leaves in mist;
but if the sun comes through it's irridescent, a
camouflage of sunlight on bright leaves. There
"he" was based: green clad, a wide-brimmed hat, red neckerchief . . .

Pearl Lagoon . . . Huahua Lagoon . . . and Sandy Bay . . .
Long sandbanks where beneath the moon
the Carey turtles come for love-making.
Punta Gorda lighthouse at 100 feet above the sea.
The Bay of Monquibel by Punta Mico.
And on these cays are coconuts. And on these coasts

are lobsters. The water blue, white cays
      (covered with white guano) lined with coconut palms.
Mico River. The Siquia. I can still see the dugouts—
      that's where the rubber-tappers go.
There too the brightly colored "dawn bird" sings.
League upon league of coconuts along the Atlantic Coast . . .
Canoes and motorboats which cut through glassy waters
           that soon revert to mirrors. . . .
A tiny village on a sandbank with a lonely lighthouse,
the surging of the waves, plop-plop of an electric generator
palm trees which sway in the sea breeze
         the moon behind the palm trees' silhouette.
The forest trees are felled in summer and the logs are marked
with paint or iron and dragged by tractor or oxen
to the gullys, to be swept down to the sea
by the first rains. I'd like to watch the lumberjacks at work.
To talk to turtle-catchers on the cays.
This is the land I sing. My poetry belongs here,
like the trumpeting *zanate*, or the wine-producing palm.
      I feel a longing for those eastern swamps.
And grow nostalgic when I think of Prinzapolka.
The bay blue with a (banana) boat at anchor in the bay.
      Banana groves along the riverbank
        with plains behind
     lagoons like *quetzal* plumage
and then one reaches Sumo Indians' huts:
      a love song in the Sumo tongue, or in Miskito.
      And in those channels, sharks.

     Ay la United Fruit!
     Ay la Standard Fruit!
Companies have passed through here like cyclones.
There have been Sundays when Miskito girls
went naked to the (Baptist) church
Miskito girls who had no clothes to wear.
And people have quite literally died
of hunger here.
          Brother Pedrón Altamirano!
When I think of the sad light of miners' lamps
I see the gold which travels down a side stream of the Prinzapolka
going on its way to vaults of Wall Street banks.
It's Wall Street that the "sun bird" sings against in Prinzapolka!

The struggle was a national one, Sandino said
                    adding that it would be international one day.
In Mr. Spencer's gold mines they X-ray
each miner twice a year
to see if he shows symptoms of TB.
If there's a shadow, he's paid off
at once. In due course he spits blood, and tries
to claim: "In good health when dismissed"
he'd caught the disease later. No, the mine
is not responsible. And so he dies on a Managua sidewalk.
(If he is a Sumo or Miskito Indian he goes home, infects
his village. Whole villages have been wiped out this way.)
Companies have stripped the Coast like locusts:
bare stumps where pinewoods used to stand.
Nothing will ever grow where they have been.
Here Magnavox passed through.
            Attracted by the scent of raw materials.
In the words of that president of General Motors
"what's good for General Motors is good for the United States"
and vice versa.
        Imperialism says it wants to make us happy!
Great forests on both banks, and in between
            the river like another (liquid) forest.
Suppose it's a Miskito settlement that we have reached
and a Miskito love song that we hear, with the word love
        kupia-kumi = "one-single-heart."
"One-single-heart": the military and money look like that
today (but those two have no heart). No: the sole true *kupia-kumi*
is Love, namely the union of the people to achieve
the Revolution. Only Love is truly "single-heart."
Not: Caribbean Bener Lumber Co. Bluefields Lumber Co. Gold
Mining Co. Luz Mines Ltd. American Smelting & Refining Co.
Neptune Mining Co. Long Leaf Pines Co. Cukra Development
Co. Nicaragua Lumber Co. the list seems endless
Magnavox the list seems endless
                        General Sandino
        the Marines are at the hut!
at the hut to rape the girl!

You brother walk unshod but you own tungsten.
Illiterate brother with antimony mines.
        I.T.T. is on the prowl

like a jaguar seeking whom it may devour.
                    (That's as certain as
that General-You-Know-Who likes raping little girls
more *campesinos* get chucked out of helicopters
                    Monsignor Chávez still keeps blessing the régime!)
Did someone say the Minister of Economics would protect
his people, rather than Esso?
                                        The *encomienda* system still survives.
And when the bell rings daily to halt dealings
on the New York Stock Exchange you can be sure that they
          have taken something from you brother which you did not even
know was yours. When Wall Street dealers say: "We dropped
five million cash this afternoon"
          that means in Wall Street parlance that they bought
five million dollars' worth of stocks and shares.
Secretaries of State may come and go like migrant birds
but Standard Oil remains.
The Canadian said to the Miskito: communism is bad
it takes all that we own. And the Miskito (who listens to Radio
Havana in Miskito) answered: bad for you, got everything
          good for Miskito
               he not got anything.
          It would be international one day
Sandino said. He also used to tell the *campesinos*
"One day we are going to win. Should I not see it
the little ants will come to tell me in my grave."
Darío prophesied, triumphantly received on coming home,
a yet more glorious country, in a toast to youth, poor good Rubén:
"I drink to lasting victory for this land of ours" . . .
(that was in 1910, the next year—1911—saw
the coming of the bankers).
          The fight is with us still: Sandino versus the Marines.
How many chopping brushwood in the hills might match Darío?
Hut dwellers in perpetual night.
          The bootblack who might have been a great philosopher.
The goatherd a great painter. Not only
               just not knowing how to read or write:
                    not even how to think, wish, dream.
See those buses laden with the poor? They're the true owners
          they put up the Bank of America building—
who the hell knows how tall?—and they (who else?)
the bridges and the reservoirs. All they need do is take things over.

The poor. Above all
the very very poor
("that fucking load of stinking shit-eaters").
A flight of jets stains the blue sky, and don't you know
that they've excluded you from civilization, brother?
yet it's your lemon grass which gives—though you don't know it—
the citronella which those jets require.
Your golden hardwood used to make truck floors
your lignum-vitae for propellers pulleys and . . . Oh well . . .
    Play me this song on your guitar
            Things do matter
            but people matter more
One suddenly comes on the camp, beneath mahogany
and ceiba trees: huts. With fireplaces, and earthenware
jars, stones to grind corn, beds of rawhide, strips
of salted meat, a carbide lamp in front of a St. Anthony,
calabashes closed with corncob stoppers, a young child crying
in a sisal hammock with bright-colored tassels,
the sounds of a victrola, and a guitar,
Sandino reading *Don Quixote*, in the open air, by firelight.
    The camp remote as any *quetzal's* nest.
Now Sandino is back on the Chipote once again, *muchachos*.
    Once more attacking Telpaneca in the night.
Pedrón once more down by the Coco
            unless he's near Boaco.
Again the peasants leave cornstalks unsnapped
            black kidney beans unthreshed
to join Sandino and besiege the mines rout the Marines
set fire to Standard Fruit Co. offices.
    A misty night without a moon: one
hundred and forty Sandinistas take the sentries by surprise . . .
Or Sandinistas lying in evening ambush on the track
down which Marines will come:
            Miguel Angel Ortez looms up in the night
black-trousered with a head of long fair hair
rifles machetes 2 old-style Lewis guns and shouts of
VIVA SANDINO! (between shots) and PATRIA LIBRE O
    MORIR!
The mist dissolves, no Sandinistas there . . .
One evening when the Marines were just about to enter a pine
    forest
        (and they did hear the throb of a guitar through trees) . . .

A sudden challenge in San Rafael del Norte from the guard post:
"Halt, who goes there?"
"Friend! Long live Nicaragua!"
"Advance and give the password friend!"
"Thou shalt not sell thy country!"
Pedrón joins forces with Ortez again to fall on Jinotega
Pedrón going from village to village once again to say "Don't use
your vote!" After one ambush the Marines could hear good-byes
mules trotting carts that clattered off into the night
but Lee fell wounded . . .
            Soon: *campesinos* running great co-operatives
                  the campaign against illiteracy
            and youngsters from Muy-Muy will get their ballet school
theatres in Tecolostote, in Telpaneca. How clear the vision
of a land where exploitation
is abolished!
      The country's wealth shared equally
the total G.N.P. an equal share for all.
      Nicaragua without the National Guard, the new day beckons!
A country without fear, with no dynastic tyranny. Sing loud, *zanate*
                  sound your bugle call.
      No beggars   no prostitution   no politicians
It's clear there can't be freedom so long as some are rich
so long as some are free to exploit others, free
                  to steal from others
so long as there are class divisions there's no freedom.
                  We were born neither to serve our fellows
                        nor to hire them
                  but rather to be brothers
each born to be a brother to the others.
Capitalism: men buying/selling men what else?
      What kind of journey brothers can we take
            while some still travel First and others Third?
There is nickel waiting for New Man
      mahogany waiting for New Man
            thoroughbred herds waiting for New Man
            the only thing still lacking is: New Man.
                  Come *compañeros*
tear down the barbed-wire fences.
Break with the past. Because the past was never ours!
      . . . those who'd still live off brothels.
As that girl said, in Cuba: "The Revolution

32

is above all else a matter of love."
     I'd like to see billboards by the roadside here:
               Your worth lies not in what you take
               from others but in what you give
—2 a.m.: San Rafael del Norte, thickening mist,
Sandino going to the church with six companions
to marry Blanca. He with pistol riding-boots red neckerchief.
Blanca in white, with veil, and coffee blossom garland.
The groom went back into the hills through mist and coffee plants
     in flower.
               Those were the days when people sang
               The buzzard is already dead
               they take him to his grave
Each tree, each bush, each rock could suddenly
               turn out to be a Sandinista sniper.
(Hunger isn't just a matter of *tortillas* and black beans
               although it's **also** a matter of *tortillas* and black beans.)
And a poster saying
     that those who died for the people
          are gloriously risen in the people.
What does the "throat-cut-bird" proclaim, or the Just Judge,
perched on the barbed-wire fences? A new dawn
and new production contracts.
               From each according to his ability
                    to each according to his needs.
A system which understands and meets the needs of life
          production determined by the needs. Example:
clothes made not in order to make money, damn it,
               but in order to clothe people.
And all luxury homes will be expropriated
               all those incapable of work
shall have their needs met by the state
                    (*The Tupamaro Program*)
Words of the *Popol Vuh*: "Let all the people rise!"
There's so much corn to plant so many kids to teach
     so many sick to cure and so much love
to give and so much song.   I sing
a country waiting to be born. The lake part blue, and partly
          silver partly gold. A flight of herons
               in the sky
"in truth it flows with milk and honey" (said the explorers)
and Jeremiah later: "Tell it to the islands

and in the dance teenagers shall rejoice"   (Jer. 31: 10–13)
Our own New Men.
Our own New Men are all we lack.
                    ("*Ye shall enter the Promised Land but yet not all*
                        shall enter")
Communism or the Kingdom of God on Earth which is the same.
General Genie's "interrogation" chambers shall become
rooms where little girls may play with dolls
and small boys with Pinocchio
            tanks turn into tractors
and police vans into high school buses
      and the machine will then be man's best friend.
General of The-Free-Men
            the little ants will come to tell you in your grave!
      What days those days when boys shall have Pinocchio
(and when my dream comes true there'll be no rich)!
Let's go and write this slogan on the walls
                LIFE IS SUBVERSIVE
or else

                LOVE IS THE AGITATOR
or the last words of Leonel Rugama (guerrillero) to the Guard
            SURRENDER?   ME?   UP YOURS!
or write these lines by Pasos on the walls
                Go home, go home, go home,
                Yankee, go home, go home!
When a *curré* calls on a dry pole that means drought
      but when he calls on a green one rain is near.
Tear down those fences and
let all the people rise, even the dead.

This is the land of which I sing.
Hoarsely, like the *guardabarranco*
      which at a distance sounds just a bit like cattle lowing,
he builds his nest in holes in rocky canyon walls.
And like the cheerful *güis* in Nicaragua's parks and orchards
the *cierto-güis* which keeps repeating CIERTO-GÜIS
      or like the *guas* in Chinandega and Chontales
which sings in the dry fields, announcing rain
thus too my song. . . .
And like the "lion bird" (or *cocoroco*) a lonely fellow
      which sings in anguish to announce a puma.
And like the "clock bird" singing out the hours

34

or the Atlantic "sun bird" saying that dawn is here
thus do I sing. . . .
And I sing like the bird they call "swamp-snorter"
(because it snorts in marshes and in swamps)
but also clearly, like *zanates* bugling
        zanatillo zanatillo
            the bird of the oppressed—
or like the "creaker" (grating in damp woods)
or like the *ché-ché* of the northern hills (guerrilla hills)
        which sings CHE-CHE CHE-CHE CHE-CHE
And like the "happy bird" whose song means FEELING JOY
the poet's voice sings FEELING-JOY
                    JOY   JOY
And I am also like the sad *cocoyo* at twilight
        so sadly singing SCREW-THEE-TOO
or *tecolotes* (owls with enormous spectacles)
        which hoot among the ruins.
Or like the *pijul* which, when rain is near,
        sings out PEA-HILL PEA-HILL PEA-HILL
among the *sorocontil*'s yellow flowers on the San Juan
near Coronel Urtecho's farm   PEA-HILL PEA-HILL
        (announcing rain)
or like the "six-o'clock bird"
        which sings a sad song in the wilderness
but only at 6 o'clock each afternoon
           when it will not stand out
   thus too my song.
Or like perhaps the loveliest bird on earth:
the *quetzal* of the misty forests—
        yet more lovely in the sunlight than the shade—
its alarm note is a harsh CRACK that's audible for miles
its territorial song is a melodious (2-tone) whistle
       it repeats
           and repeats.
To give A.P. the lie (and U.P. too)
        that also is the poet's task.
"Like certain birds which only sing for certain races"
as Joaquín Pasos said.
                There are
                problems
                only when
                there are solutions

"One-single-heart"

                    PEA-HOOL PEA-HOOL PEA-HOOL
                                         PEA-HILL
          JOY JOY
                         CRACK!!!
          I-SEE-THEE

                         GO-LAY GO-LAY
               SCREW-THEE-TOO   SCREW-THEE-TOO
          CHE CHE
     MARY DAWN IS HERE / MARY DAWN IS HERE

1972   [R. P. -M.]

MOSQUITO KINGDOM

The coronation ceremony was in Belize this time,
the king riding on a white horse in procession to the church
with the uniform of a British major, the others on foot
with red frock coats (castoff) of British officers
of all ranks and wearing sailor pants.
His Majesty was placed on a seat next to the altar
and the coronation rites were performed by the chaplain
acting on this occasion as the Archbishop of Canterbury.
When they reached the part that says: "And all the people said:
'May the King live forever, long live the King'"
the frigates shot off their cannon, and the Indian
and black vassals shouted: "Long live King Robert!
God save the King!" His Majesty meanwhile
seemed absorbed in looking at his lace. After the anointing
he kept touching with his finger the holy oil (which was
castor oil) and then putting his finger to his nose
but he did not flee in the midst of the ceremony to climb a coconut
      tree
as his illustrious ancestor had done in Jamaica.
After the ceremony the crowd
went to the schoolhouse for the gala banquet
in which no food other than rum was served
until King and court rolled dead drunk on the floor.

Vanderbilt never in his whole wretched life had had a vacation
and this time he determined to have one in Europe and therefore
a special ship was built. No one had ever seen anything
more fabulous on earth. The newspapers were stunned.
No private yacht could be compared with the *North Star*
in size or luxury: 2,500 tons; 300 feet long;
enormous paddle wheels moved by two motors. And the
walls of the vast saloons: of marble and granite.
The coffered ceilings of rosewood and sandalwood; in the ceiling
medallions of American heroes; the staterooms
like the apartments of Cosimo de'Medici

(even though his carpet in Washington Place was frayed)
and with a great cargo of ice, wines, rare foods, famous
chefs from New York, and a chaplain who blessed the food.
This time Vanderbilt "spent without his usual inhibitions."
In London the *Daily News* saluted the floating palace
with an editorial. He was given a reception in Mansion House
with many flunkies and with Carlyle. The Lord Mayor drank a
      toast to
"Mr. Vanderbilt the foe of monopolies" and Vanderbilt
made a speech—the only time in his life that he did so.
He saw Victoria and Prince Albert only at the Opera.
But in Russia Czar Alexander lent him his carriage
and Grand Duke Constantine, his son, inspected the ship
and asked permission to make a sketch of it. Emperor Napoleon
      (Louis)
paid him no attention because he was busy with the Crimean War.
They did not open the Tuilleries for them and Mrs. Vanderbilt
did not see the wardrobes of the Empress Eugenie. Summer on the
Mediterranean . . . King Bomba of the Two Sicilies . . .
      then
Greece, etc., and the millionaire got bored and went back home.

But the British agents got screwed because the monarch
began to sell great portions of his kingdom
for barrels of rum.
In 1839 the sovereign "in the fourteenth year of his reign"
(having already sold a third of Nicaragua
half of Costa Rica
and a limitless stretch of Honduras)
was forced by McDonald to make his will
naming McDonald and others as "Regents"
in case His Majesty should die before the Heir Apparent
came of age
and shortly after this the King was kind enough to die
and his Eminence Colonel McDonald published a decree
in the name of the child king George William declaring
". . . the said surrender of territories null and void . . ."
because the grantees obtained them at a time when the king
was bereft of reason [drunk]." But the decrees of one king
were worth as much as those of another, and one Shepperd, an old
      British
sailor, almost blind, in his Greytown house (San Juan del Norte)

years later still kept in a cupboard those old papers, with
   "X his mark"
          (because the sovereign couldn't sign)
of King Robert Charles Frederick,
that made him the owner of a third of the Mosquito Kingdom
("We, by our special grace, do give and grant . . ."
from Bluefields Bay to Colombia (Panama)
a total of twenty-two million acres
and a Texan named Kinney, who speculated in cattle and enormous
chunks of Texas, acquired the moth-eaten papers of the
sea-wolf through the promise of a half million dollars
(the biggest real-estate speculation in his whole life)
and he organized a so-called Central American Company
with authorized capital of $5,625,000 and 21 directors
and two hundred twenty-five thousand shares at $25.00 a share;
each share would bring 100 acres of land
on being presented at the company office in Greytown.
On Wall Street they believed he was a partner of Walker
but he was more a rival.
"I have land titles to begin legally," he said.
"I'm going to create a government and the rest is easy."
President Pierce, it was said, was on his side.
But the "Transit Company" was not . . .

In New York he recruited 500 men to capture Greytown
but before he could do it he was shipwrecked opposite Greytown
he reached Greytown shipwrecked and bankrupt to boot
with only 13 men and a printing press that he saved from the wreck.
But even so he had himself elected civil and military governor
by the handful of lazy inhabitants, in "a democratic election"
and he organized a provisional government while they were drawing
      up
the new constitution inspired by that of the United States.
Ten days later the press began to publish
the newspaper (bimonthly) *The Central American* with ads
for commercial firms in Greytown, import & export houses,
hotels, schools, bars, lawyers, banks,
clubs, doctors, bookstores, nightclubs, etc., etc.,
to attract immigrants. Alsop & Co., on California Street
(Buy and Sell Exchange) . . . Benicia-Boarding School
for young gentlemen—*The Atlantic Loan & Security Bank*
          The Ocean House (. . . on a romantic Lagoon . . .)

CAFE FRANÇAIS (every kind of refreshment)
to attract immigrants to that place which was nothing but
a swamp with 50 houses (thatched roofs) and 300 inhabitants
of all colors, nearly all blacks (ex-slaves from Jamaica,
fugitives from justice, and an occasional European) on the shore of a
noxious lagoon, full of alligators and surrounded by the forest,
a place that had been described as "one of the saddest
and most desolate on earth . . . so much so that, however varied
the experiences that the traveler had had with lugubrious places
the memory of Greytown would stay with him
as among the most melancholy and dismal . . ." The only banks
were sand banks covered with shark bones
that obstructed the sea view. The lively dance halls,
the lively dance halls of *Delmonico's* (open till dawn)
were probably the frog-filled swamps.
The monkeys: perhaps they were the music at *Mike's*
("Visit Mike's—The Best Restaurant"). Language Schools:
the cockatoos! *The Green Resort* perhaps wild boars
and tigers. Royal Caribbean with its enchanting singers
the Jamaica Grill, Jimmy's Café, so many more puddles
(or the luxurious St. John) with crocodiles, with mosquitoes
("Make your reservation . . .") but the immigrants did not arrive.

Vanderbilt had given up the presidency
of the Transit Company when he went to Europe
and he had made Morgan president and while he was traveling
Morgan and Garrison had made the shares fluctuate
earning enormous sums at Vanderbilt's expense
and he (who said "I don't give a shit for the law,
I've got the power") when he came back just sent them a note:
"Gentlemen: I will ruin you. Sincerely Yours,
Cornelius Van Derbilt"
The Transit Company had never paid Nicaragua
the 10% of the profits claiming that there weren't any profits
and Nicaragua couldn't claim that there *were* profits
because of the peculiar way the company kept its books,
which consisted of never recording either passengers or cargo.
Toward the end of December '56 the bar of the Hotel St. Charles
in New Orleans had more noise and more cocktails
than usual because the steamship *Texas* was leaving
with recruits for Walker toward the lands of the sunny South,
the hot, sensuous South, with the laudable intention

of robbing them (but those who went to Nicaragua almost never
    came back)
Italians who fought in Novara, Prussians
from the campaigns in Holstein, Englishmen from the Crimean War,
Yankees from the expedition to Cuba . . . (They carried the rifles
    in boxes
shaped like coffins.) And on the very same seas of Kidd
    and Morgan—
the other Morgan, the pirate—they would scan with their telescopes
the western, wood-covered coast of Cuba
saying that it would "sooner or later belong to Uncle Sam."
(And when they got to Nicaragua they would open the coffins.)
    Morgan
and Garrison who were losing control of the company
courted Walker so that he would confiscate it from Vanderbilt
who had never paid anything to Nicaragua, which now belonged
    to Walker,
and would deliver to the two partners the dead corporation with
a new contract that would set them up as a new company.
A plan of unscrupulous captains of industry against
a rival equally unscrupulous. A shark fight
like those of the reef of San Juan del Norte. There was stupor
on Wall Street when they learned of Walker's confiscation.
Panic among the investors. They all rushed
to sell their shares. On January 1st they had been at 18,
on February 14th at 23¼. On March 14th (when
the news arrived) they went down to 19, and on the 18th, to 13.
    In 4 days
15,000 shares changed hands. Vanderbilt, wounded,
attacked Walker. Oh, the bastard, said Vanderbilt
I'm going to screw Walker. No more boats to Nicaragua.
And as Morgan and Garrison weren't ready with theirs
the filibusterer with the gray, empty eyes ("that in daguerrotypes
seem to be without eyelashes") and a mouth that under no
    circumstances
did anyone ever see smile, was left trapped in Nicaragua.

The immigrants didn't arrive. And the British agents
didn't recognize the "provisional government," and besides
Walker was now in control of Nicaragua, and Kinney had no funds
    anymore
and besides he was ill, and many of his followers

went off with Walker. For some months he vegetated in Greytown.
Then he went away sick and without one cent.
              Sick and penniless.

Afterward Vanderbilt sold his ships and snapped up railroads,
              and forgot about Nicaragua.
His wife asked him: "Aren't you rich enough?"
        "Not yet."
Just about then a newsboy ran by under his window on
Washington Place shouting: CIVIL WAR!

The newspaper from San Juan del Norte with its fantastic ads
is disintegrating in the Library of Congress in Washington,
the librarians say, and it can't be Xeroxed; you touch it
              and it turns to ashes.

1972   [D. D. W.]

ORACLE OVER MANAGUA

In back of the yarn and textile factory (if there's anything left
of the factory after the earthquake) and next to the drainage channel,
near the lake, among rubbish, broken chamber pots,
are (or were) the footprints, stamped in volcanic layer.
Perhaps before there was any weaving, or even any pottery,
they occupied this area of Managua together with the bison.
They lived by hunting and fishing and growing crops.
          Tiscapa, Asososca, Nejapa,
the present lakes were a single smoking volcano
and ashes once fell like a black snow
and the footprints were left in the stream of volcanic mud
that was flowing toward the lake and solidifying under the ashes:
footprints of people all going one way—toward the lake—
          footprints fleeing from the volcano,
some more sunken (it shows that some were carrying loads)
          not running (the steps are short and even),
and there are tracks of white-tailed deer, otters, lizards,
and a bird called guan (*Penelope purpurascens*)
and bison tracks . . . Down upon them came the black rain.
Afterward another stream of mud, and another black ash.
Then thick streams of mud (several of them): all this
a thick layer of stone—years—that later would be
Managua building materials. A short period
(decades) of volcanic inactivity (patches of earth and
beds of extinct rivers). Later a more distant volcano
(Masaya?) threw off a rain of pumice stone. Once again
stillness (a yard-thick deposit of earth).
Other eruptions with currents of khaki-colored mud.
Another deposit of earth built up. More mud
from eruptions, and finally the top layer of earth
with the first pottery. Maya. Monochrome. From Nicoya
(polychrome). From the time of Christ. Moon pottery
(white lacquer and fine-lined motifs). Charming
red jaguars with a white background, incense pots. And on top
bits of Coca-Cola bottles and Goodyear tires and chamber pots.

Acahualinca begins there, the houses of cardboard and cans
        where the sewers empty . . .
                Streets that smell of jails,
that characteristic jail smell,
of shit and rancid urine
houses of cement bags gasoline cans rubble old rags.
                The sewers end there.
On the shore of the lake the kids play digging little holes
with a little stick to see who'll get the most flies out of his hole.
In the water cotton swabs, toilet paper, a condom or two.
Nearby the slaughterhouse. Buzzards sitting on its scraps.
A stream of dirty cloudy water flows toward the lake
to the right the poisoned soft-green lagoon of Acahualinca . . .
huts in the plain where the D.N. trucks dump
(or used to dump) Managua's garbage
a plain of cans papers plastic glass skeletons of cars
buzzards perched on dry posts waiting for more trucks.
                Other sewers empty there
without reaching the lake   (the moonlight shimmers on the
        shit).
        There the children with wary little eyes
the children weak sickly enormous beetles
        their bellies swollen and their legs thin as toothpicks
"And when night comes he goes looking for warmth
        it's a joy to see him eating dirt"
Old women crouched over the guts that the slaughterhouse throws out
scaring off the buzzards.
        The pig and the pot-bellied kid in the same puddle.
The old women now squatting at water's edge, near the drain, washing
        the
guts they'd sell in the Central Market for sausage meat.
I saw a papaya tree in a street like a miracle in that horror.
The faces of the people, smiling, but covered with flies.
Above cardboard roofs and rubble a picture-postcard lake.
Victims of a permanent tremor, these people will have
no planes bringing canned foods,
medicines, tents, drinkable water.
                The woman who gets attacks is there. Her husband went
                        away
in a truck and never came back.
        One guy earned his living selling sawdust and a truck ran over
                him.

44

Far off there, beyond these pigsties, on the pier
Darío with his marble shirt against another picture-postcard blue
(also polluted)
"with the force of the diarrhea the tip of his little asshole sprouts"
            "All night long it's just one wail
if they turn her over on her side the rumble of her little guts
sounds just like they were emptying a slop jar"
            "He's just crazy about dirt"
            A moon over Acahualinca
with astronauts on it singing Frank Sinatra songs
      The current flowing slowly toward the lake
the current of Managua shit
and in it prints of bare feet
like the feet of the people who went along there fleeing
ten yards deep as if it were now in fresh mud.
            "Apollo 11, this is Houston . . . Over"
      sky black as midnight and glittering earth
      and the shadows of the craters black as the sky
      and the beautiful earth, blue and pink, in the black sky
      like an oasis of life and color in the empty vastness
            ("the most beautiful of jewels")
but to the poor like craters and lunar seas
"Blessed are the poor for they shall inherit the moon"
The woman that lost her sewing machine and then her husband
(he became a drunkard). Her roof of Standard Oil cans.
And the other one heavy-breasted from suckling her children.

Up there, "The Hill," on what was left of that volcano.
" 'You dumb kid, why don't you confess?' They tie
my feet again . . ."
In the ruins of the volcano that made the ancestors flee
the palace with machine guns trenches tanks cannons
like the prehistoric eruption terrorizing the people.
            Now which way do we run?
            Looking down on all of Managua.
                  Tiscapa: at the edge of the crater
                              the power.
            At the edge of the crater the ancient terror.
All night long those lights shining.
The reflectors reflected below in the volcanic lagoon.
            A howl of wild beasts in the dawn.
" 'He won't confess.' Now to gain time . . . More time. I cry out

begging for mercy. No, there's no mercy. Back to the water.
That same night a boy stripped to his shorts.
      Like one of those frightened puppies.
'Drink it up,' said Colonel Somoza Debayle to me. 'Isn't it
your own blood? It won't hurt you.'
I began to confess lies, my voice faltering, the stenographers
getting it down on paper with their swift pencils . . ."
      Between one torture and the next one he'd see a movie.
   "They put me in a cell called the Tiny One
opposite the electric plant of the Presidential Mansion
at its highest part the cell is three and a half feet high
at its lowest part it touches the floor. From there
I saw the tortures. They were from midnight to two every night.
     Major Morales squeezed my balls."
". . . They took me to the garden, where I'd seen Narváez in the
panther's cage in pajamas and barefoot
   and other men in the lions' cage
now Narváez was in with the lions
    and Julio Velázquez in the panther's cage"
(It happened next to the pool, next to the cabañas of the presidential
    pool)

From my house we could hear the roaring at dawn.
When they were hungry. Each dawn. Somoza's zoo.
At that time we didn't know the prisoners were in with the animals.
The black panther had been a gift from Castillo Armas,
which was not very soothing, you might say. Somoza
fat and all decorated like a Christmas tree.

The seminary students used to take a walk to Acahualinca to see the
    footprints.

And so you went underground
    and died in the urban guerrilla fighting
All life unites
        unites and does not divide
   (it integrates)
For that you gave your life, you
on the fifth planet of a medium-sized star of the Milky Way.
    Great feelings of love
    at the risk of looking ridiculous—Che had said.
Every living substance unites.

What is fecundation really?
Every living substance: fusion with what is different
                unification with the opposite.
Although death is as ancient as the cosmos
                        the antiprotons fight the protons
                        the antineutrons fight the neutrons
                        antimatter fights matter.
And now with bazookas they try
                to stop history.
"Verily, verily I say unto you
                the Revolution is in the midst of you."
It's suicidal not to try it, you used to tell your friends
in the India Coffee House.
In the midst of the general tendency to disintegration
                there is an inverse tendency
to union. To love.
                Our poor aqueous systems
clamor for union—a solution
based on water and salts, energy in the form of carbohydrates.
                An inverse tendency which is the Revolution.
That's why you Leonel Rugama a twenty-year-old poet
became an urban guerrilla fighter.
Ex-seminarist, Marxist, in the
India Coffee House you used to say that the Revolution
is communion with the species.
                Announce that the kingdom of God is at hand.
As a male sperm cell penetrates the female ovum . . .
That's why you fought all evening in that house.
                After all God is also City
(God as City:
        The City of the definitive meeting
of each man with all men
the City of identity and consummated community
                the City of Communion)
For the sake of that City you became an urban guerrilla fighter.
                It is also like a mustard seed.
The Revolution is also like a cell that splits in two
                and each one of those two becomes two others, etc.,
and like a male embryo that goes on growing.
                The transformation
of monkey into man, of course.
                Since the first carved flint.

47

Texaco, Standard Oil . . . The monopolies
will be extinguished like the dinosaurs of the Jurassic Age.
And Cuba used to have 25,000 whorehouses
            or 27,000 I don't remember.
        Revolution means to change reality.
Let us, Leonel Rugama, organize hopes.
Possibilities that can't be dreamed up by computers.
            To make real the Kingdom of God.
It is a law established by Nature
that no molecule can permanently retain
            more energy than the others—
The economy of the future will be to make life more beautiful.
If we knew nothing of the metamorphosis of the insects!
A new society
                a new heaven and a new earth
also the production of free time
and with the development of production capacity
the development of the inner life
            a new man and a new song
that's why you died in the urban fighting
            a new man to dream new dreams.
And in Cuba words have vanished like
bayú (whorehouse), *capataz* (foreman), *criada* (maid), *chulo*
    (pimp).
Also *garito* (gambling den), *fletera* (prostitute), *garrotero* (money
    lender).
        This is almost not a poem.
I mean: there are words that young people in Cuba do not know.
            The Jurassic dinosaurs disappeared
                and they were the superior beings of the Jurassic Age.
The life of each one richer, more beautiful.
Evolution comes in leaps, said Mao,
                evolution is Revolution
            Revolution is not illusion
                the caterpillar weaves around itself a new home
                from which it emerges with colored wings
                with which it flies off to the sky
You, Leonel Rugama, bullet-riddled and carried off to the morgue
            stained with earth and blood said *La Prensa*
you were the light at the end of a tunnel.

And why is it expanding, for whom is the universe expanding,

the flower becoming bigger every second?
                1,000 light-years are like a quick kiss
(and the opposite)
And Revolution is a function of evolution itself
because   /leaps as Mao says/
        evolution has a frightening velocity.
                From a little stick came light.
First came the conquest of fire in the Pleistocene Age.
Cold night changed into days in the depths of the cave!
Some deciphering the sky . . . the phases of the moon.
Science was born in caves. And organization
                (the mammoth could be hunted only co-operatively)

Later on better than raising sheep was stealing sheep.
                War could be an industry.
To guard the wheat as important as sowing it.
                War could be productive.
And after domesticating animals man invented a way
to domesticate man.
                Not killing the enemy: making him work.
Slavery the basis of industry and the accumulation of capital
        (rows of fettered people on the Babylonian seals)
as important an invention as the domestication of animals.
Afterward not just enemies: the poor man could be sold.
Or the exile. One could go to Egypt
to become a slave. The pyramids begin.
                And if there are slaves—others no longer work.
The archaeologists find two kinds of tombs.
(In the Neolithic village the tombs are all alike.)
        And consequently the dwellings.

The division of classes a product of progress? Yes
but it did not accelerate, it retarded future progress.
Progress in Neolithic times was in the production processes
                and it was made by the producers
but now these—the inventors—become
the lower class. Inventions were labor saving:
        plows tools sailing ships . . .
The invention of slavery makes inventions superfluous.
No more saving of labor, no more inventing of anything.
(Slavery, then, as the retarder of progress.)

49

I know good, decent people who
            imagine the future as a repetition of the present.
She was as skinny as a little frog . . . They say to her:
"But you're so skinny, you look like a little frog."
"It's because when I didn't get many men
they'd punish me and wouldn't feed me.
That was awful, they even made me sleep
with ugly guys, guys with smallpocked faces."
"And how much did they sell you for?"
"La Pichula sold me for 300 pesos."
            76.4 million for the processing units
            90.6 million for installations
            13.9 million for concessions
            46.7 million for contractors
            The refinery has . . .
"To import equipment and raw materials without duty, and
to export products also without duty . . ."
Let the archbishops tell the people, these are your oppressors.
Animals of the same species do not devour one another.
And you really thought Christ would *come back* to earth.
That one day there would be joy forever.
The City at the end of history
            where matter will no longer be ephemeral.
        ". . . a new heaven and a new earth . . ." (nothing less?)
(So you probably say that Marxism is "utopian"?)
        The transformation of the caterpillar into a chrysalis and the
            chrysalis
                into a butterfly.
In short: Nature must be distributed to us
            by the New Man whom we already love . . .

If the history of humanity were 24 hours
                        let's say
private property, classes, division
into rich and poor: these would be the last 10 minutes.
        INJUSTICE/ the last 10 minutes.
(The top layer of earth with Mayan pottery and Goodyear tires.)
            So all the great subconscious
            is Communist.

There were almost no arms (arms of war, that is).
Militarism does not coincide with the great inventions.

Organized war came after the inventions.
(Agriculture, pottery, weaving, the sail, the great
invention of bread . . .) Nor did it contribute to the increase
of the species.
Each invasion destroyed what had been built, it burned, it razed.
Militarism retarded, made man retrace the traced.
Science exploited by superstition.
Kings and priests at the expense of farmers and artists.
(Magic as the origin of authority/dictatorship.)
                    All this
has had to go from the classless society of the past
to that of the future.
"ARMS FOR WHAT?" shouted Fidel to the crowd
(1960 A.D.) in Santiago de Cuba.
Arms for what? We are attending the burial of arms and banking,
my friend.

They could leave the *campesinos* on their land, even
protect them, in exchange for farm produce (tribute)
and the *campesinos* then produced more than necessary—
to pay that bribe that was maybe more than what was left
for himself—and this created an "aristocracy," a
class that lived off the *campesinos* and took from them
more than they needed for their own consumption and so they had
a surplus of things to pay for the development of other things
for consumption (by the same aristocracy) or commerce
            and so there were rich and poor.

We enter into the Easter of the Revolution.
After the bombardment of words and bombs
        the slow sale of lives (hours/ months/ years)
fecundity sabotaged and beauty sabotaged
after the terror in the streets filled with radio patrols
        the Central Intelligence Agency
        anchilostomiasis and equisistomosis
the United Fruit lush as a cedar of Lebanon,
the burning of huts, the boot on top of the pregnant belly
        and baseball to make the people forget
(this is the paschal mystery of the Revolution)
we shall be reborn together as men and as women.
        It becomes a chrysalis and the
                chrysalis sprouts wings.

Evolution taught the species lessons
for survival. Union: it was one of the most important.
        Class divisions and war
were not evolutionary lessons.

Sowing crops was not invented without co-operation, without
the union of a few men
and they didn't invent speech without co-operation,
or flocks . . .

Man forgot the ancient lesson with
private property and the accumulation of capital
        the ancient lesson of survival
the principle of equality that gave such good results . . .

Drinking coffee in the India or the Hotel Santa Cruz you used to say
that the inner revolution and the other are the same.
(It's because the universe and the heart are one. Or just as there are
within the cell the orbits of the solar system.)
Also saying that all revolutions are
a single great revolution. As you were in the seminary
you said that the revolutionary "is a militant saint."
Also talking of "the sanctifying force of the revolutionary."
You called the underground, when you entered it, *catacombs*.
And the seminary was also a kind of underground.
    The harshness of that struggle. There you also looked for
a kind of guerrilla warfare. Also
           not to commit suicide, or
said in another way: to die for others.
        Whoever saves his life will lose it.
You knew how bloody the inner revolution is
(less moving than under the machine-gun bursts
high in the mountains with the red sun and Camilo up ahead)
      Brother Lorenzo 30 years in a convent kitchen.
Revolution is at times routine and without glory.
Che knew that struggle, too.
                —condensed milk and rotten cat flesh—
And when you were an acolyte in the insane asylum: the madmen
    covered with crap
        and the Mass smelling of shit.
            And also the humiliation
of wearing, in this heat, a black Sadducean cloak

when they walked two by two to Acahualinca to see the footprints.
He who does not hate his father and his mother and lovely girls . . .
celibacy, a Sierra Maestra or the Long March.
That's why afterward you could preach (India Coffee House)
"freedom is our DEATH but with it we give LIFE"
or "the fear of delivering ourselves up to a sacrificed life . . ."
"the duty to make the Revolution without even hoping to see victory"
    Che knew that braver struggle
      "farts, vomit, and diarrhea"
says the diary. Without glory, shit-covered in a hammock
    they lent him a pair of pants
"but with no water I stink of shit three miles away."
I imagine your seminary:
      Monotonously
a choir rehearses psalms in a remote Gregorian chant . . .
And a remote John Chrysostom: "You who are man, a most gentle
  animal
(you used to read his Homily)
you shut up in your house the food of a thousand hungry men"
and from the seminary you look (or used to look) at all of Managua,
the middle-class center, around it proletarian homes,
on this side Acahualinca, close by the insane asylum with the poet
  Cortés,
Managua (still) between the feudal castle and the lake
and in the center, white, as high as the interest rates of the Central
  Bank—
a billboard on the highway ENJOY—
    around where the madmen are.
Another kind of warfare . . . Perhaps a worse underground.
But you also knew a revisionist Gospel
    The Bank of the Holy Spirit inside the Vatican—
     Banco di Santo Spiritu—
God's Bride a prostitute, the Bride prostituted
Generale Inmoviliare part of the Patrimony of the Holy See
or rather Generale Inmoviliare a Branch of the Vatican
and Vittorino Veronese, that's the name of the mamma's boy
President of Italian Catholic Action and the Banco di Roma,
    the Church goes to bed with anyone at all.
And more than half the bishops in Nicaragua were apostates
    and His Most Craven Excellency that night,
a sad night, anointed with trembling oil in the stadium,
poor old man, Somoza's daughter as Queen of the Army.

The gold crown belonged to the Virgin of Candelaria. And Somoza
uniting house to house and estate to estate. And the shouts
of the harvesters mounting to the ears of the God of the Armies.
And they said in the Curia: "No, not with a signature! With a
    mortgage."
        The priests of the Curia: "No, not with a signature! With a
            mortgage."
Monsignor Borgia all in red tassels and phylacteries
            presiding over the Bishop's Conference
                "And that prick from Nazareth, what's he saying?"
    . . . the apostasy of the Nicaraguan Church . . .
        "Changing it as many do"
(to the Corinthians: that he did not "negotiate with the message
changing it as many do")
            That money should be the source of money
                                that is the great sin.
Fernando said: don't fuck around.
Tinita Salazar doesn't earn ten pesos a week.
Pijulito died because the hospital wouldn't let him in.
            And then they talk to me about God. Don't be ridiculous!

As for Acahualinca, you felt guilty. Innocent!
            those people are innocent!
Some of us are mass murderers; others are
like the guard who turns his back so as not to see the torturing,
and he lights a cigarette.
5 years in the Seminary. Seminarist and then Marxist.
        And God? Well, what about God?
                Let's make a distinction:
there are many Gods
                the God of John D. Rockefeller . . .
You were looking for communion,
        communion with the species.
        After all, to die for others
was not an act of scientific analysis but an act of faith.
        The Paschal praxis.
And Yahweh said: I am not. I shall be. I am the one who shall be,
He said.
I am Yahweh a God who waits in the future
    who cannot be unless conditions are fulfilled
        a God who is not but who WILL BE

for He is love-among-men and He is not, HE WILL BE)
We shall know God when there are no Acahualincas.

And you would ask yourself the big question:
                what are we doing here on the Great Ball.
"He who has two robes let him give one to him who has none."
                Man as an end in himself . . .
Father Blanchart, O.P., says that
the Church of the future will have only revolutionaries.
A new man   a new time   a new earth
                The heart of man and not the structures?
To change consciousness without transforming the world?
A classless city
                the free City
where God is *everybody*
He, God-with-everybody (Immanuel)
                the Universal City
the City where God's humanity will be revealed to us.
                A million years without private property
                        and only 7000 with private property and
                                rich and poor.
And what more?
Che insisted on going back to Havana that evening
        and the pilot said No because of the bad weather
and Che kept insisting and the pilot said No, bad weather
and the fact was that Che didn't have the money to pay for hotel
        rooms
                for himself and his guests
(and Che was president of the Bank of Cuba).
"So human as to approach the best of what is human . . ."
Impossible with money or arms to prevent
                        the expansion of the universe.
We are beings who will achieve human dignity.
It is a priestly struggle said Father Camilo
        And you said: "Let's sow it!" (life)
"Without expecting any notice in the news or in history."
                The dough rises.
                With yeast the dough rises.
The dough rises. The great loaf lifts itself.
Common ownership of means of production and distribution.
The commoner it is the holier it is said Saint Gertrude.
And Clement of Alexandria: They will not be saved unless they make
        restitution.

Injustice, in the last 10 minutes
            10 minutes, 8 minutes
"the widow, the orphan, the poor man, the foreigner"
It is a law of nature that there be no division in the same species.
        If there are 50 people and only one bottle of water
            there is a fight for it, if there is
one bottle for each one there is harmony
                (so abundance is important).
"And if they ask you for the moon?" Sartre asked Fidel.
"If they ask me for it it's because they need it."
            To make out of each man a man.
Let poets be agitators and let lovers be agitators.
Stone Age . . . Bronze Age . . . now Age of Love.
Man's greatest crime is to prevent men from being men.
            Only 10 minutes ago, 8 minutes.
It's not certain that it's since "the world has been a world."
A consumptive dying on a sidewalk. This was
before the earthquake. He had been a miner
in the Neptune Gold Mining Co. at 10 cents an hour
and he said: the silica was so fine it looked like smoke.
            Sandino used to say: I won't live long.
And around Matagalpa, the so-called night blindness (from hunger)
as soon as night falls they're sightless, groping in their huts,
their pupils dilated, until the next day, at dawn.
            The most perfect being in the solar system.
That's why you went underground, and as you wrote:
        "with no alternative to fighting."
Subversion as a moral imperative. And you understood
that fighting as meaning not to commit suicide.
            Antihistoric regimes roaring all around.
Julio was the chief of the underground.
            They'd like to see the evolution of the universe slow down
that's God's honest truth
the rest is publicity and public relations
a merchant who says we're here to serve the customer.
Easier a camel through a needle's eye
than development with the Interamerican Development Bank.
            "Apes of the darkness of this world" (Paul to the Ephesians),
businessmen, executives more pernicious than typhus,
good women worse than gangrene,
                                minority,
        microbes in the mystic body
                    create antibodies.

A system that forbids us to love
(there might even be the danger of a chilling of the planet.)
Or as the boys say now:
                    It's absolutely hopeless.
You used to come in old clothes. Laughing
you used to come to the *La Prensa* office with your poems. Joking
with Beauty just as you did when as a kid
you squatted down to see the teacher's panties.
          Writing was as simple as taking a bus.
      Verses to the rose are not middle class
      and roses aren't middle class either
            the Revolution will grow them, too
            it's really about distributing roses
                              and poetry.
And poetry
was also going in a barge along the Siquia—
                    the barge with the jukebox—
and seeing the water the color of a Shaller Cola bottle.
The ooze on the wetlands; strips of old quilts.
A bridge that the tyrant inaugurated in the movie house by cutting
    a ribbon.
A girl washing, breasts seen from far away (coffee-color-people)
(Or the girl that always goes along the opposite sidewalk and doesn't
    nod
but she goes into the poem that Pablo Antonio will publish in *La
    Prensa*)
          Lies and more lies on the teletype
our battle on the field of language
          the ugly they make beautiful and the beautiful ugly
      truth is a lie and good is evil.
Literature, as effective as guns—said Mao.
They are advances in the common language, the language of
      liberation
the language, you know, that makes Latin America one
      and its Revolution one.
The explorer bee with dance and song before the beehive
shows in which direction and how far away the flowers are
          (a function of the poet in the community)
. . . guns, according to Mao.
          You wanted poems for the truck driver
(in the India, the little Santa Cruz Hotel) for the bootblacks
                              But

(Shall we do better to wait for others to free us?)
the hand of the love epigrams turned on a light.

Those farewells are for keeps Julio had said.
Bastards! You later saw the house in the Frixione quarter
full of smoke and with holes blown out by Sherman tanks
(you noted down: "Sherman," "Browning," "M–3," "M–1"
                             to include this in the poem)
where he had fired all alone against hundreds of guards
tanks planes security agents enlisted men supply
trucks—firing all alone from the balcony.
He fired all afternoon. Steady shooting on both sides.
And the tank with its cannon. The light planes. Helicopters.
And they thought there were a lot of them, and it was just one guy,
    all alone.
The radio interrupted the news for a soap ad.

             With no alternative to death.
You went underground
            or as you said, you entered the Catacombs.
Nights when all lights are suspect
nights sleeping fully dressed on the floor of an empty house
with the M–3 at your side
tiptoeing to peer behind the blinds with cocked pistol
       (you see ghosts everywhere said Julio)
and it's only a couple making love in a car.
                  Julio also said
You think I'll let myself be taken alive by those sons of bitches?
Sometimes maybe women guerrilla fighters listening to rock on the
    radio.
      It was after the assault on the Bank of America.
Selim Shible, Silvio, Casimiro, Julio, they had fallen.

Behind the clandestine blinds you could see the bootblack
             an ice-cream vendor
        the lady that peddles chitlins
                  chitlins! chitlins!
the dried tripe peddler (they're going to have a Shakespeare reading)
a man selling greens, shouting greens!
a man selling firewood, a man selling coal.
Other poets get drunk or go whoring. You died.
          DEATH to give LIFE

They say you wanted to form a group of guerrilla poets
to show that "intellectuals can throw their weight around."
            Target shooting because we had
to kill the hunger that's killing us, that's what you said.
And then one day in *La Prensa* an 8-column headline
SANDINO NEST DESTROYED WITH MACHINE GUN AND
      CANNON FIRE
There were three of you. 18, 19, and 20 years old.
You were the oldest. Security agents reached
the sky-blue house opposite the East Cemetery
Ephraim's mamma shouted: "The guards!"
            the first volley and two guards fall
more patrols, and more bursts of guerrilla machine guns
and more guards fall, Garand rifle fire
                        reinforcements begin to arrive
jeeps buses from Transit Headquarters big jeeps
from the Combat Battalion official cars trucks
from Security more guards with rifles or machine guns
hundreds of spectators watching the fighting like at the movies
a light plane was flying over the house, higher up a helicopter
the sound of the bullets against the walls of the house
inside cheers for Sandino
at four a tank arrives firing cannon shots
a cloud of dust over the house when the tank would fire
            something began to smoke
the cannon of the tank was also smoking
            more shooting, and nobody knows how many there are
            inside
or what weapons they have
cheers for Julio Buitrago
            the guards bring hand grenades, the boxes
set down with great care (Photos) Turn
to p. 12, to p. 18.
from the Combat Battalion official cars trucks
answers again
            other shots from inside
another cannon shot from the tank.
      The bullets from the plane against the zinc roof
the bullets scattering the tree leaves
ambulances wailing like wounded animals
soldiers behind lead-colored jeeps, khaki-colored jeeps
firing at the windows, the corner house newly painted

sky blue, firing and shouting orders to surrender
new reinforcements along West Cemetery Ave.
and the boys shouted: "A free country or death!"
The shots striking against the Acapulco Barbershop,
against the Esso Station, against the little market
        a kid was picking almonds in a nearby tree
        and he observed the whole battle from up in the tree
the guards firing and firing from behind their jeeps
and the guns jerking with each shot
and the crowd not knowing who's inside
answering the army's fire. The guy in the gas
                station falls shot in the foot
        (he was watching from behind a post with his legs spread)
the guards now filling the streets, the corners
guards still several blocks away
some crawling toward the house with hand grenades
a priest insults them, rifle thuds, they've arrested Father Mejía!
        La Prensa goes on (see photograph)
The kids shouted son-of-a-prick at the guards
and they went after them with fixed bayonets
        others shouted behind them and they turned around
and you too were a kid who played ball,
who played jacks on street corners and pitched pennies
on the bricks of the park paths, always the lucky one.
        Another cannon shot and more shots from inside.
Yours was the "first stage" (destruction)
        which, you used to say, always has a "touch" of grief.
Shots sound from inside, more
Garand rifle shots against the house
the plane passes over again
        again the ratatat of the machine guns
                with no alternative to death
near your little park where, as a kid, you played ball
and jacks and where the Firuliche Circus of your childhood raised its
        tent,
        a tent all patched, and
where the old market women would go and crap in the bushes
your childhood neighborhood, everybody listening to soaps
and anti-Communists, the poor things, after so many years of radio
years and years of the daily news . . .
        The guards fall back. A silence, and then
the great explosion . . . another . . . and another

they were shoving people off the streets
and a new cannon boom
a little girl of three to the reporter "I was scared
real scared of the pistol when it went bang bang"
Another volley from the tank of the Armored Battalion
    with scarcely an answer from inside
The articles and the photographs are there
the *chanson de geste* was a newspaper gone with the wind.
    The house now all riddled with gunshot and cannon shot
sporadic gunfire now
        shots from inside (feeble)
Crack . . . Crack . . . Crack . . . Silence. Another grenade
      And a guard shouts: "Lay down your arms, you're
          surrounded!"
it was then, they say, that you shouted:
      "Let your mother lay down!"
and now there were thousands of spectators watching the movie
people, heaps of people, the people for whom they were dying
"The plane God it splashed the little house from top to bottom"
Chola Paz's little kids ran bare ass into the street
    And the other woman who said she thought they were
      firecrackers
but she saw the guard. She and the kids went into the bathroom
    SING NATIONAL ANTHEM BEFORE DYING
"We were inside the bathroom but even in there we could hear
when the boys began to sing the national anthem"
I report this from an old newspaper gone with the wind
      Not until dusk did the guards occupy the house
a patrol entered the house in ruins. A silence
of five minutes. A burst of machine-gun fire
and then total silence. An officer with a machine gun came out
and gave the cease-fire order. "All three of them are dead!" he
   shouted.
      A backed-up truck
              and three corpses tossed into the truck
black shoes and a pair of dirt-colored arms
the body of a long-haired blue-jeaned red-shirted boy
and the other one red-chested—what the reporter saw.
The Acapulco Barbershop was left with its mirrors smashed.
    "Rake arms!"
The Army Bulletin:
      "three M–3 machine guns, three 45 pistols

and a 9 millimeter caliber pistol"
                    (that's what the guerrilla fighters had)
The hundreds of guards began to rest arms.
Demolished doors twisted iron zinc roof
riddled by the plane the walls with great gaps
blood in the patio a blood-stained mattress in the bathroom
shreds of shirts, underwear, handkerchiefs soaked in blood
blood in the kitchen beans on the floor, pot lids
with great smears of blood in the patio the house full of smoke.
Like those animals that die after intercourse . . .
            (A photograph of a mother in mourning leaving the
            morgue.)

They had to die for the sake of the chitlin peddler
            "chitlins! chitlins!"
for the sake of the woman peddling dried tripe
        another form of life now lifeless
"Nicaragua is a nice deal" says the *Oil and Gas Journal*
for the sake of the peddler of cold fruit juice and the crackling
        peddler
        your death, or rather your resurrection
for the sake of the consumptive lying under the tree and the whores
        in the whorehouses
and the pretty girl that used to go by on the opposite sidewalk
always the opposite one. The rhythm of the stars is the same
as that of the cells. And for the sake of the dusty soap-opera
        neighborhoods
            with walls on which a kid is scratching
                asshole cunt prick

Now from the seminary you can see another Managua
a few seconds and all the pride was shit upon
shells of houses like rotten scorched eggs
smoldering walls
            windows like eyeless sockets
Managua surrounded by a huge concentration-camp barbed wire
its decomposing body breaking into bits
        buzzards over the City Bank.
Another Managua: block after block after block, leveled flat!
    "Behold I make all things new"
floors stuck together like playing cards
above the rubble of a nightclub the remains of a sign

a huge television ad above other ruins
    Here were the showcases filled with toys
        . . . a smell like a dead rat . . .
    Here's where Sears used to be
movie houses with bellies burst open
demolished the great hospital that rejected Pijulito
"This is the Avenue of the Army?" "No." "Then what was its name?"
a sign THE COLISEUM. Could it have been a restaurant?
The blood bank that bought the blood of the poor
        plasmapheresis "at a good price"
the stadium, the Somoza Stadium it was called, once full of fanatic
    fans,
the one where a girl was anointed that night as Queen of the Army
    (what an Army!)
    the mansions of the rich with their Nativity scenes in the living
      room
the Country Club where the Bashan cows used to drink Scotch
        the office buildings went down in thirty seconds
        Announce it in the palaces of Assur
        Tell it in the palaces of Egypt
the address book now useless
        and the telephone directory
the Bank of America skyscraper was a torch in the night
    Pepsi Cola was flat on the ground
the Grand Hotel as if bombarded by Sherman tanks
the Air Force Prison without walls or prisoners or guards
    the American Embassy on its knees
the Luis Somoza statue hollow toppled to the ground a stump
like one more corpse dug up from the ruins
          Up there, "The Hill," now uninhabitable
Security lurching on Tiscapa Lagoon
the torture chambers slithered toward the lagoon. The great
tower rolled to the waters of the lagoon. With one slice
missing, the wedding cake of the Presidential Palace,
Somoza's messages on the ground, the wind ruffling them, with
fragments of china, the one that was so often featured in *Novedades*,
in the distance the Combat Battalion barracks razed
and the Armored Battalion: tanks crushed beneath the concrete
and *Novedades* was pulverized
that dawn Hughes fled
like a bat smoked out of his hiding place, without

63

organizing his chain of casinos.
Something more than an adaptation movement of terrestrial layers.
On the sidewalk the 5th floor of the Communications
Building (it was the telephonic censorship one)
a geological midwife or whatever you want to call it
that night the Sandinistas went free
the Courthouse tilting and shattered
the banks dynamited, downfallen
all the religious schools—they were only for the rich—
the temples, all of them! there they celebrated false rites
liturgies that turn God's stomach
A Christmas Eve without stuffed turkeys.
And there are no streets now
"the horrible starlit night"
(See the *La Prensa* account three months later)
the dead carried on planks, on doors.
Lightless, foodless, waterless Managua—
all a great Acahualinca—
like the night when there was no room for them in the inn
all Bethlehem celebrating its Christmas Eve supper—
the sewers erupted
chaos blood pillage—Their idea of Communism
those who never used to pray prayed, the Christians didn't have time
a home delivery of the Last Judgment
what we thought could be seen only somewhere else or on TV
there was no room in the morgue
the National Guard looting like an army of occupation
with the groans of the wounded and the wails of the ambulances.
But   "Can there be a catastrophe in a city
if Yahweh didn't order it?"
the arms exploded like roman candles
The House of Pellas lit up like a Christmas tree
the only banks now . . .
are blood banks
the stars are shining up above.
The roofs collapsed with all their ads.
This was Roosevelt Avenue . . .
You can still see ITT KODAK.
A Santa Claus among the rubble. All squashed
the cars more cherished than the children
eyes to see not and ears to hear not
the twisted letters A NEW YEAR/A NEW CAR

a mass of tiles rules mud and bricks
a Christmas wreath still hanging on what was once a store
at 12:27 A.M. all the Christmas carols and commercials were
    silenced
        bricks adobe twisted iron
all the streets lost, all the familiar routes
                blackened ruins
avenues of glass concrete desks and building blocks strewn about
        a smell of dead rat everywhere
strongboxes overturned, a sign
                      "The Barber of Seville"
just when the Christmas sales were so good in
the luxury shops over which the bulldozer is now passing
                      PURCHASE . . .
    mutilated mannequins ballet slippers bidets
    everything dragged off by the tractors
    television sets freezers washing machines
        —You ordered your prophets not to prophesy—
the homeowners lost all their homes
all equal now
        the subsoil released its energy
                none of her lovers comforts her
alas, the beloved city, the city of private property
your prophets announced for you falseness and stupidities
into the lake they go on throwing bricks TV sets safes
(the IOUs charred) smashed furniture cars
all the things that the workers made
flowerpots rugs suits juice squeezers
but they were sold to them as though they belonged to somebody else
everything that the tractor goes on carrying away record players toys
nobody could afford cash registers caviar cribs
    the breathtaking velocity of evolution, this is
a terrestrial prelude of revolution.
The story of the farmer who took his little daughter to see the center
    of town
        "look, child, so you'll never believe in these things."
For Pharaoh and his technicians they were only "economic setbacks."
        And they still tell us not to prophesy.
We're under Martial Law, don't prophesy.
And there'll be still more horrors to come.
Hours earlier some young men had begun a fast in the Cathedral
placards "Food for the people of Acahualinca" and
        "A Christmas Eve without political prisoners"

Two ways of looking at a plague:
the point of view of Egypt
                    and that of the Hebrews.
Ruins, ruins, ruins without one electric light
in all those ruins
            the huge Christmas tree still in Republic Square.
It's sad to think
we'll never see Bolivar Avenue again
                    The black ruins in the moonlight.
I got to know a place here called Volga Delights.
        This was my city
where I'd go in the afternoon hand-in-hand with Adelita
        avoiding the center of town
through pink side streets where there were always buses parked
and we would pass by groups of drivers.
        Paris Bar Fatima Boarding House India Coffee House.
The black ruins and the intermittent
explosions of the demolition in the dark.
        Here there was a corner called the Little Tree.
Streets where they sold fried pork, jerked beef, dried tripe.
        The Five Sisters was a friendly bar with
a dirt floor and good free lunch (a long time ago)
and there were neighborhood directions like: From Caimana's
three blocks toward the lake and then one block up; she made
        fireworks
la Caimana and she dressed like a man and had a mustache.
The Poor Man's Mandarin was a railroad workers bar.
                    In charcoal on a board wall: We've gone to Manuela
                    González's.
Here there used to be whorehouses
                    boards stones earth
whorehouses homes stores inexpensive board and room (Meat
        Tamales for Sale)
all alike
        stones from the volcanic strata of those footprints
        of Acahualinca with which Managua was built
the moon behind the wire fences and the explosions
Bolivar Ave. where I saw her for the first time
(many years ago dressed in yellow)
rumbles from the buildings that they're dynamiting.

We shall weep not for this rubble but for mankind

66

yet death is born with the body and it *dies* with it
    death is the death of the individual
    a "touch" of grief
to be reborn you must die
        (you loved the future and you died for it. You accepted
        this touch before these people, brother, your death is dead).
Pitiless midwife. At the Chevron Gas Station
a man was stroking his daughter's face as if to lull her to sleep
        (like everything that cannot die
        you then went on to live in another form).
Blessed be those with liberating grief.
    "Remains."
The people went off in trucks with their stuff, their junk
the people took to the highways
the people never dies.
                "They left in the midst of tears
                but I make them come back happy."
And the symbolism of these tents.
Conditions propitious, for what? (Question mark)
With the earthquake capitalism sank deeper into capitalism.
    Some of the guards had a lot of fun getting people
    to run after the food trucks and from time to time
    tossing out a few cans.
Means of production not to be in the hands of a few bastards.
Are they going to halt the march toward the promised society?
                One class I shall save
                    and another class I shall destroy. Oracle of
                    Yahweh.
Nobody knows when it will come into being, said Lenin (Paradise).
    The people are untouched
they clean up the rubble and transform the gruesome city
the rebuilders of the city working just for food rations
go late at night to the outskirts to sleep and a few hours later
they regroup in squads and march off to the rubble.
A boy of fifteen—just for food, mind you—and the marquee of the
    movie house fell on top of him.
But the people are immortal. They come smiling out of the morgue.
The chewing-gum sellers the paper boys the car watchers
junkmen knife grinders are everywhere, they are the *foundation*
    if *they* shake the skyscrapers fall.
Trains and trucks go out loaded with cotton pickers
the huge gleaming granaries are empty, filled with hunger

                    (or Somoza rice)
their laughter in the warehouse facing the bay and throughout the
    countryside.
Your barge goes along the Siquia again with piles of beer
crates full or empty . . .
    and our crime is to announce a Paradise.
Monopolies are only since the Neolithic Age.
    The Kingdom of God is at hand
the City of Communion, brothers.
    Only the dead are reborn.

Once more there are more footprints: the pilgrimage has not ended.

At midnight a poor woman gave birth to a baby boy in an open field
    and that is hope.
God has said: "Behold I make all things new"
    and that is reconstruction.

1973   [D. D. W.]

TRIP TO NEW YORK

That afternoon I thought I was still on my Solentiname
    island
instead of peering out a plane window over New York Harbor.
Ships down below, barely moving, my plane just as slow.
    The rush-hour traffic jam at Kennedy Airport
forced us to circle over New York for an hour.
What miracle has put me above Manhattan this late afternoon
circling skyscrapers reddened like the clouds?
From the seat beside me (vacant) I picked up a *New Yorker*
"This week Washington awoke from its Watergate stupor."
Senator Fulbright fears they may fall into a totalitarian system.
Ladies and Gentlemen: Kennedy Airport is still jammed up.
As I press against the window bent over the water of New York
    Harbor
    the plane, as if anchored to a cloud, doesn't move.
Ad for an island—swimming pool tennis cottages water sports
    The Island Company Ltd., 375 Park Avenue
Cartoon of a fat man with a newspaper saying to his wife
"All these years of struggling and the *Times* is *still* calling me a
    'reputed Mafia leader'"
Ladies and Gentlemen . . . we've now been picked up by radar and
we're heading straight for Kennedy Airport on automatic landing
factories, trains, little suburban houses all alike, matchbox cars,
and finally on the runway. Along with a hundred more planes
    like sharks.

Waiting for me was young, bearded Gerard, who miraculously
brought me to New York and tells me to call him Tony,
we're riding in his poor old car toward New York, rivers of cars,
he invited me to a benefit for the Managua victims
but he needed someone to pay the fare, he says.
    He finally got it, God takes care of everything. He works
with orphans, drug addicts, poor Puerto Ricans
and while he was in a ghetto, he got the idea of a benefit for
    Managua

he needed a hall, was turned down at Columbia, looking up at the
  sky
he saw the Episcopal Cathedral of St. John the Divine, walked in
            and the Bishop said to him, "Why not?"
      New York prisoners gave pictures they painted
      North American Indians also gave woven things and ceramics
more rivers of cars trains trucks, superhighways all crisscrossing
            he's a Catholic he tells me and also a Zen
he'd worked before at St. Patrick's Cathedral, he couldn't stay
      on there
                  its present cardinal worse than Spellman
along the highway messages from gas stations drive-ins motels
      a car graveyard melancholy in the twilight
some hippies have camped in the Gethsemani monastery, he says
guys with girls too, the abbot allowed it
in the United States monasteries are getting emptier and emptier
young people prefer small communes. I tell him
that Merton used to tell me those orders would disappear
and only small communes would be left
            the sky smog and ads
                  rectangular hulks among the exhaust fumes
and most all the contemplatives, Tony says, have a mentality that's
bourgeois   middle-class
indifferent to the war issue. And to the Revolution.
            LIQUORS   DRUGSTORE
"You think New York's changed a lot?"
I was here 23 years ago. I say: "It's just the same."
      The rows of red and green traffic lights
      and the lights of the taxis and the buses.
            "Madison Avenue" says Tony. And laughing:
"It's funny: Ernesto Cardenal on Madison Avenue." And I look
at the deep canyon, the sunken gorge of buildings
where *the hidden persuaders* hide behind their windows
      selling automobiles of True Happiness, canned Relief (for 30¢)
            The Coca-Cola Company
we cut through the canyon of windows and trillions of dollars.
"For centuries they didn't eat meat; now that many of us are
      vegetarians
they're eating meat" he says. From a street corner the Empire State
      (just its bottom floors). At the heart of Imperialism.
"Famous monks come to lecture on asceticism and
  they stay at deluxe hotels." And now on the West Side

Cafeteria—Delicatessen—Dry Cleaning
We arrive at Napoleon's apartment, 50th and 10th Ave.
Along the sidewalk, blue-jeaned and blue-eyed teenagers
clustered around bicycles, or sitting on the steps.
The doorbell doesn't work but Napoleon and Jackie were
        expecting us.

Napoleon Chow of Chinese and Nicaraguan ancestry
and Jackie is an anthropologist, a specialist on Turkey.
The little apartment monastic, but with Persian tapestries.
I call Laughlin at his home in Connecticut.
Surprised: "What the devil am I doing in New York?"
He laughs clear from Connecticut. He'll come in on Saturday so we
        can see each other
at his place in the Village.
Napoleon and Jackie do yoga. On many days they fast
completely, other days they cook very well, eating
                Chinese, Turkish, Nicaraguan food
("food as joy; sacrament")
There is an Angora cat that shits in the toilet just like people.

Tuesday evening, the Cathedral of St. John the Divine
110th Street, opened its bronze doors for the exhibition.
    I read my *Oráculo sobre Managua* (the Earthquake part)
among prisoners' paintings and Indian ceramics.
A full-bearded rabbi prays: "Our guilt
in such tragedies . . ." And the Dean of the Cathedral: "Our
        System,
Lord, which aggravates those catastrophes . . ." (And I'm thinking:
        the Somozas
                a 40-year-long earthquake.) Benedictine Brother David:
"And Lord it is in New York of all places
where you gather us from different countries and religions
to pray for Managua, and to meditate
                on how much ought to be destroyed here"
Dorothy Day was ill so she couldn't come.
María José and Clemencia, two beautiful Nicaraguan girls (I met
        their father)
ask me how those streets were left (I met him once
that April night
                we were on our way to storm the Presidential Palace,
Chema, he was tortured and murdered)

I just tell them: "I met your father"
In the choir loft, slides (radiant colors) of the Debris.
Corita (ex-sister Corita) gave 6 paintings to help Managua.
          Daniel Berrigan is expecting me tomorrow.

Central Park (uptown): And I tell myself: that's where the swans
          are.
I remember my Liana, and the swans.
She got married. The swans must still be there.
Once, one hungry day, Louis trying to catch a swan.
Once again I saw people talking to themselves in the streets
          "The Lonely Crowd."
With Napoleon and Jackie in Times Square, nothing to see
and along 48th Street among the titillating porn movies.
          An empty store, 2 policemen taking notes
               its window front shattered, and no one looking (right on
               Broadway)

With Daniel Berrigan at the Thomas Merton Center
Daniel (Dan) in blue-jeans and sandals like me, his hair
          "a street kid's hair after a fight"
and the same smile he flashed in the pictures as he was arrested
by the FBI (jubilant between the glum FBI agents)
     he'd read my *Psalms* in prison.
Also there, Jim Forest (a pacifist) with a big mustache
younger than I thought. He wrote to me once.
He told me that Merton gave him a crucifix that I made in
          Gethsemani.
     He's in from Washington, from a protest march
from the Watergate Building to the Justice Department.
And Berrigan sitting on a desk, his lean face propped
on one knee, and his thin hair in his face. Barely recovered
from jail, they tell me. And a girl:
     "The tortures that *aren't supposed* to take place in the United
          States"
This is a group of contemplatives and resisters, says Berrigan.
     Meeting one night in a Harlem convent
     they got the idea of establishing this Merton Center.
They study the mysticism of different religions
                    including the American Indians.
"Merton suffered horrors in the monastery" says Dan
     and all of us know it. And Jim reminds us about

when he was forbidden to write against nuclear warfare
because it wasn't a monastic theme.
Dan: "He told me he wouldn't ever become a monk again
but being one already, he'd go on being one."
"He was going to go to Solentiname after Asia, wasn't he?" Jim asks.
    And Dan: "And are you sure he isn't there?"
And Dan also:
" 'Contemplation': it's an awful drug we have here.
They meditate. Without thinking at all about the war. Without
        thinking
at all about the war. You can't be with God and be neutral.
True contemplation is resistance. And poetry,
gazing at the clouds is resistance I found out in jail."
I tell him he ought to go to Cuba. He says he's still on probation.
    I also tell him: "In Latin America
we're integrating Christianity with Marxism."
And he: "I know. But not here.
        Here it's Christianity with Buddhism.
Jim, by now aren't we all Buddhists?
Isn't there any Buddhism in Latin America?"
                                            "No."
Tomorrow, at the Merton Center, they're celebrating
the wedding of his brother, Philip, the other priest,
and ex-nun Elizabeth McAllister—and we're invited.
Philip splashed blood on the draft files in Maryland
then Philip and Daniel burned the files in Catonsville
with home-made napalm (a soap-powder-gasoline mixture)
and Jim also napalmed the files in Milwaukee
        (and they just got out of jail)
They say Merton once considered such an action.
    There's a girl fasting because of the Cambodia bombing.
        On the wall a Berrigan poem about Vietnam
        on big sheets of paper put together like a mural.
When I leave, Dan gives me a fat loaf of bread
a great round loaf of whole-wheat bread, baked there.

To the movies with Napoleon and Jackie for a Cuban film
Memories of Underdevelopment
        They don't idealize the Revolution
a documentary segment—a writers congress—
    And I believe I saw Roque Dalton in the documentary
Fidel delivering a speech (and part of our audience applauds Fidel).

A crowd of people on the sidewalk arriving in evening clothes:
   the Opera.
            Tony's aristocratic Italian grandfather
            left him a villa on the outskirts of Rome.
He's probably going to give it to someone. He doesn't want to own
   property.
And Tony said: "Holy Communion . . ." (with burning eyes)
"Communion is my greatest union with people each day. For me,
Communion is the most revolutionary thing in the world"

Philip Berrigan and Elizabeth McAllister
accused by the FBI of plotting to kidnap Kissinger.
      Their wedding celebration is at the Merton Center.
Contemplatives and radicals, pacifists, many of them ex-prisoners
            Christian Anarchists and Christian Buddhists
and, at this party, a Eucharist with protest songs
            sitting on the floor
after the Gospel, Jim and Dan talk, and a young lady
who's just poured blood on Nixon's dining table
and smeared the dining room walls with blood, on a *tourist tour*
of the White House (the press never reported it). She is pregnant,
awaiting trial and maybe years in jail.
Dan Berrigan consecrates a loaf of bread like the one he gave me
and little glasses of wine. The broken bread passes from hand to hand,
      and the wine.
Then a collection . . . for the poor Watergate defendants
            "enemies and *brothers* of ours."
Back to the party. Dan says: "No more religion."
Gallons of California "white wine" and "rosé" on one table
raisin pudding, apple pie, cheese, on another table.
A very long-haired blond young man, Michael Cullen, greets me.
He used to read my *Psalms* in prison, he says,
and I've read about him.
He hands me a pamphlet he's giving out: *If Mike Cullen Is Deported*
He was born on a farm in the south of Ireland; he came at age 10, not
to make money. He studied at a seminary. He got married, sold
      insurance
but he was troubled by the rat-infested apartments
   and the blood gushing in Indochina
he burned his draft card. Along with Jim
he burned the draft files in Milwaukee
   the cards marked 1-A to burn bodies in Asia

now they want to deport him, he believes they'll deport him he says
    sadly
someone passing by stuffs some money in his pocket and tells him
    "keep going" and he smiles (sadly)
he tells me: "The American Dream has become a nightmare."
All the TV cameras on Philip and his wife.
"I believe in the revolution" he says "My contribution is nonviolent"
Blue-eyed Phil. Husky like a football player
            "the Gary Cooper of the Church"
Elizabeth's sweet: she says they've married to help each other in
        the struggle
and they'll create a commune to help others carry on the struggle.
            Dan with his radiant smile
            and his Zen peace

Leaving the Doubleday Bookstore, on 5th Ave
a few men and women in white tunics dancing on the sidewalk
and the young men with shaved heads (in white) look like Trappist
        novices,
            In a shop window:
    Mink. A Persian Lamb Leather Jacket.
    A brooch of diamonds and rubies . . .
A young fellow with a campaign button on his chest: IMPEACH
    NIXON
            Plastic women.
I cross the street in fear: WALK—DON'T WALK (in red)
The clerks in the stores almost all Cubans
and it seems to me that I'm hearing talk
    by revolutionaries.
The sky filthy. Police sirens.
Old women talking to themselves.
Coronel was telling about that French Dominican here, who told him:
"Since I came 3 months ago I haven't been able to say prayers."
Museum of Modern Art. No time to stop in. And what for?
Frank O'Hara used to work here. He wrote his poetry
            on his lunch hour—sandwiches and Coca Cola.
We once wrote to each other.
Now I've bought his *Lunch Poems* ($1.50) at Brentano's
and the cars remind me of his death
    Run over in New York (on his lunch hour?)
            WALK—DON'T WALK
Dorothy Day expects me at the *Catholic Worker* says Tony.
On the telephone, she remembered she'd once written to me.

A "paperback" bookstore on 5th Ave.
Many books about the Indians. Pawnee. Sioux. Hopi. The Hopi,
anarchists and pacifists for 2000 years, Gandhians having never
    declared
war or signed a treaty (not even with the U.S.A.)
and now I'm on my way to a noon meeting with Kenneth Arnold
my editor for the English *Homenaje a los Indios Americanos*
Black Elk's autobiography is also here
            Once he came to New York with Buffalo Bill
sky-high houses, lights made from the power of thunder,
he says that here he was like a man who'd never had a vision.
Red Fox also with Buffalo Bill. He loved the Indians, he says,
he defended them in Washington. Time for me to meet Kenneth.
He's in from Baltimore. We plan to meet at the Gotham Book Mart.
I Have Spoken—I've got a copy. With Seattle's speech.
            Seattle, wrapped in his blanket like a toga
    with his well-known voice, loud and clear for half a mile,
among the tree stumps in a clearing: "My words are like the stars
that never change. Whatever Seattle says the Great Chief in
    Washington
can rely on like the return of the sun or the seasons . . ."
            Outside it's raining a rain with no smell
and it's almost lunchtime
            NO SMOKING
"And when the last one of my people has died
and they speak of my tribe like a story from the past . . ."
        whisper of tires on rainy streets
    neon reflections on gleaming wet asphalt
". . . and your children's children think themselves alone
in the field, the store, the shop, they will not be alone.
When the streets of your cities are silent and you
think them empty, they will be filled with the spirits of the dead.
Dead did I say? There is no death. Only a change of world."
I leave with books for more homages to the American Indians
and I head for the Gotham Book Mart—3 blocks away—and there is
    Kenneth.
He's young, bearded. Also there, silver-haired Miss Steloff,
the famous owner of this bookstore. And I was here once
at a party for Edith Sitwell. Miss Steloff
invited Coronel and me and we brought Mimí Hammer.
And Auden was there, and Tennessee Williams, Marianne Moore,
    Spender . . .
Kenneth brought the cover for *Homage to the American Indians*

76

and we go half a block to a Chinese restaurant, and
    the lunch was chow mein but first two ice-cold beers.
This abundance of books about Indians, he says,
goes back a year or two. Indian things have become fashionable.
He also has a poem about Indians, or rather
about Buffalo Bill, his great-great-uncle. Yes, the brother of
    his great-grandfather was
    Colonel William Frederick Cody (Buffalo Bill)

Tony comes by for me, and he apologizes for the car.
His fell apart. This luxury car belongs to his dad. (Ashamed)
We're invited to lunch by Brother David's mother
(with Napoleon and Jackie). An apartment in an elegant section
of 5th Ave. She's an Austrian Baroness
but she works as a store clerk. She gave away her money.
A girl has brought me a present: a Watergate Poster
—a mugshot of Nixon labelled WANTED
            Brother David says to me
"What would you say to the abbots about the monasteries in the
    United States?"
I laugh. "Seriously. If the abbots all asked for your advice?"
"They wouldn't take it." "But what would you tell them?"
"That they should become Communists."
A girl: "Why society first
instead of the heart? What's inside comes first!"
I tell her: "We are social beings. Social change is not *outside* us."
            The lunch: yogurt with strawberries
            a loaf of dark bread and another even darker, milk
            blue grapes, red apples, yellow bananas,
            honey, the most delicious honey I've ever tasted in my life.
No liquor at this lunch. I'm the only smoker
            ("The air is polluted enough without inhaling more
                smoke")
Brother David talks with a small string of rosary beads in his hand.
I ask him: "Can you ever integrate Buddhism with Marxism?"
"Through Christianity. You have integrated
Christianity and Marxism, and we here Christianity and Buddhism."
        Tony leaves us to call on his orphans.

12th Street. Joaquín's apartment was around here. In that house,
        I'm almost sure.
A seller of old books in the Village in love with my shirt
        my cotton peasant shirt from Nicaragua

he asks me who invented it.
        A gold sign: MONEY. (Pawnbroker)
I ask for Charles St. A well-dressed man on a bench: Don't
know, he says. Could I spare a dollar? He hasn't eaten in two days.
        Parra was in Chile.
On every television screen Dean testifying against Nixon.

        Washington Square: Rock in the park
amps crazy electronic music frenzied announcers
thousands of longhairs howling with the band black men blondes
        black women
with the band, barefoot bearded wearing beads or rags
howling with the band, stomping on the grass or
stretched out smoking necking drinking canned beer.
A group of lesbians shouting. Beyond them with a banner,
        GAY LIBERATION
passive before the Methodist, Bible in hand, preaching to them
with a choir of wooden-faced ladies in robes down to their ankles.
        Crossing the street
two faggots with their tongues are licking
a single cone.

The studio of Armando Morales, the Fuse: in the Bowery
the neighborhood of the beggars and the *Catholic Worker*.
It's a storeroom. Without a bath (you bathe in the sink with a
        sponge
over an edition of the *Times* to keep the floor dry)
with California wine we recall pre-earthquake Managua
facing the Fuses's canvases which the Gallery is selling for $10,000.
The ashtrays, sardine cans—the kind that open with a key,
the lids rolled halfway back; and piles of those ashtrays.
        He explains to me: the Gallery sets the price, and those
are the "stocks" of a painter. A buyer of "Morales"
invests in him as in General Motors. If there's a rise in the price
(the stocks) they'll invest more in him. And if the selling stops
        The Gallery still couldn't cut prices
even if the Fuse is starving to death—the price cut would create
        a panic
among the "investors" in Morales' intricate colors and mysterious nudes.
He paints his colors, then covers the whole canvas with black.
Then he *shaves* it, with a razor blade, scraping off the black, and
he repaints all the colors over the scraping.

"Now I finally know how to paint" he says "I can paint anything
    I want.
        What's hard is to know what to paint"
We remember *Las Cinco Hermanas*, that barroom in Managua.
We remember some super-muses that we more or less loved.
And the time we found we were on the police list
    of homosexuals—he for being a painter, and I a poet.
And he remembers that whorehouse "La Hortencia" and I tell him
it wasn't where he says, it was somewhere else. And it's
    not there anymore
because later they built the Church of the Redeemer there
    (the Fuse laughs)
and I was already a priest saying Mass there until my superior
    stopped me
for my anti-Somoza preaching (the Fuse laughs even louder) and
    besides
there isn't even a Redeemer now, it collapsed in the earthquake—
    He can't give pictures for the earthquake benefit
        his painting belongs to the Gallery.
On every television Dean kept on testifying against Nixon.

Laughlin is a door-high man, and
(as I already knew through Merton) brimming with love.
After we're inside he asks his wife about Nicanor's wine.
Where's the wine Nicanor left? He takes out of the refrigerator
the Portuguese white wine, Saint What's-his-name that Nicanor left
the last time he was here. We're holding our glasses, about to drink,
when Laughlin lifts his toward heaven like an Offertory:
"To Tom, I'm sure he'll be enjoying this party
wherever he is!" And I: "He's here." Nicanor Parra's wine
is delicious. "It's a curious thing" says Laughlin "after his death
you saw that each friend of his believed he was Merton's closest
    friend."
After a pause and a sip of wine: "—And each one really was."
He chats with Napoleon Chow about China and with Jackie about
    Turkey.
He gives us a few of the latest books from New Directions.
We've quickly signed the contract for my book *En Cuba*.
More wine. Margaret Randall seems to be happy in Cuba—that's
    great.
He feels very friendly toward her, although he doesn't know her.
Then I mention that Laughlin's a good poet, I've translated him, and
    he says no

Pound told him he wasn't. He slashed through his poems
with his famous pencil. He told him: "Do something useful" and he
became a publisher. Nobody had a publisher back then, only
        Hemingway.
He was attending "Ezuversity" in Rapallo. He used to lunch
        with Pound
and his wife at the Albergo Rapales. Then swimming or tennis
and reading Villon, Catullus. Pound was his mentor.
        He tells how Somoza once stole a mine from an uncle of his.
—James Laughlin is the grandson of Laughlin the Steel King—
        "Of course he knew" says Laughlin (meaning Nixon)
Nicanor's wine is gone, so we go to a French restaurant
three blocks away.
"He liked solitude a lot and he liked people a lot.
He loved silence—and conversation, too.
Merton was gregarious, you know, and a perfect monk."

Midnight. Tomorrow's *New York Times* already at a tobacco stand
        NIXON KNEW SAYS DEAN (we buy it)
In the subway an Army poster: boys graduating—
        . . . after graduation it's nice to join the Army . . .
And the dark subway cars now go by wildly painted on the outside:
        The names of boys and girls in many colors
        Alice 95   *Bob 106*   *Charles 195*
and the express trains flash by as if they were covered with flowers
(their names and the streets where they live) "they write them
so someone will recognize them, so as to be real" says Napoleon
        painted with every color spray paint
and there are names even a yard high
        Manuel . . . Julia . . . José . . . (many Puerto Ricans)

Slums "without any beauty except for the clouds"
36 East 1st Street (the Bowery)
I was moved as I saw the tiny sign out front: *Catholic Worker*
a fat man lying on the sidewalk asks me softly for a cigarette
        I was moved as I went into this holy place
she wasn't in, but she soon came along the sidewalk with a few
        other women skinny, hunched, her hair white
she's still beautiful at 75
I kiss the saint's hand and she kisses my face.
Like my grandmother Agustina in the fifties (when she could still
        read and she was a reader of this woman)
This is the famous House of Hospitality founded

by Peter Maurin and Dorothy Day during the Great Depression
where food and shelter are free to all who come
   drunks weirdos drug-users bums and the dying
and it's also a pacifist and anarchist movement:
its goal, a society in which it will be easy to be good.
   Soon the poor would be coming in for their supper.
I was studying at Columbia, and even there we heard
that a saint had died in the beggars' neighborhood.
Peter Maurin, agitator and saint
used to preach in the parks:
                              "Fire your bosses." Or
         "Giving and not taking
         makes people human"
In his one and only suit, rumpled and the wrong size. Without a
      bed of his own
in this place that he founded, not even a corner for his books.
   He used to walk without watching the traffic lights.
And she's been devoted since then to
"the works of mercy and rebellion." A life
of daily communion and of taking part
in every strike, demonstration, protest march, or boycott.
They come here to work without wages, students, seminarians,
teachers, sailors, beggars too, and sometimes they stay
all their lives. Many have been in jail or are still there.
Hennacy used to fast in front of the government buildings
with a placard, handing out flyers and selling the paper
and he didn't pay taxes because 85% is for the war
he worked as a farmhand to avoid paying taxes.
Hugh was skinny, in shorts sandals and a poncho, and
         he also did penance in the streets.
Jack English, a brilliant journalist from Cleveland
was the cook for the *Catholic Worker* and later became a monk.
Roger La Porte was a handsome blond 22 years old; he killed himself
by setting himself on fire with gasoline in front of the
         United Nations.
And an old ex-marine, Smoky Joe, who fought against Sandino
in Nicaragua, died here, a convert to nonviolence.
         Merton worked here before he became a Trappist monk.
The paper still sells for a cent
as it did when Dorothy Day went out to sell it for the first time
         in Union Square one May Day (1933)
It was the third year of the Depression
         12 million unemployed

and Peter wanted the tabloid to be (more than a publication of
    opinions)
a revolution.
              The pots now steaming
They're beginning to come, the poor, the homeless, the Bowery
    bums,
to line up. "The other United States" says Dorothy
        men replaced by machines
        and abandoned by Holy Mother State.
Shouts. Someone has bust in kicking and reeling.
        Two *Catholic Worker* people gently take him out.
"We *never* call the police because we believe in nonviolence"
And she also tells me: "When I visited Cuba
I saw that Sandino was one of their heroes
and I was glad. Because as a young woman I collected money for
    him,
when I was a Communist, before my conversion to Catholicism.
And I saw Sandino's top generals (not him)
in Mexico: with their big sombreros, eating hot dogs
        why hot dogs I don't know"
And lively, raising her white head of hair: "I know Castro's Cuba,
as I told you in my letter. I liked it"
Shouts. Now it's a dwarf. And someone gently carries her away
    lifted in the air like a doll.
She says that now they're helping Chavez's workers by
boycotting the A & P chain. And she prays, she says,
for the United States to have a purifying defeat. She talks
about Joan Baez who used to sing in Hanoi during the bombings.
    She says
Hennacy used to say: "Contrary to what people think
it's not us anarchists that are bomb crazy; it's the government."
   And there isn't peace because the streets would be left with
        no traffic
the factories at a standstill, birds singing on top of the machines
as she saw during the Great Depression. She talks about the horrors
she has seen in the Women's House of Detention
the times that she's been in jail. And watching the poor come in
she repeats what Peter used to say: "The future will be different
    if we make the present different"
A reverent good-bye to this anarchist saint
and to this holy place where everyone is welcome, everything free
        to each according to his needs
        from each according to his abilities.

DOWNTOWN. UPTOWN. Bang. Bang. Trains thundering along
underground Uptown and Downtown
with the names of poor children painted like flowers
     Tom   *Jim*   *John*   *Carolina*
their names and the sad addresses where they live. They're
real. So we'll know that they're REAL. Bang bang
the express trains on high tension cables,
their shining ads for Calvert, Pall Mall, and the Army
     it's nice to join the Army

At night, near Wall Street, in an apartment with no furniture
Marxist priests and laymen and Protestant ministers
   "To change the system in which profit is the goal of mankind"
"There is no room for Christian ethics within the limits of private
    morality"
     "The vision of the Kingdom of God is subversive"
One of them works with computers, another with the poor.
Sunday night, and whole floors still lit up on Wall Street.
They're screwing us.
    "Hello Bogotá"
             "Hello ITT"
2 twin skyscrapers taller than the Empire State
the whole top half lit up
imperialism looming up in the sky behind the windowpanes
Hello we wanted more drought
   Who is that other monster rising up in the night?
The Chase Manhattan Bank screwing half of humanity.
Behind Wall Street, the Brooklyn Bridge, like a lyre of lights.
In the dark two kids look like they're stripping a car.
   Our pale satellite above the Brooklyn sky
      flattened like a football.

Early the next day Tony took me back to Kennedy Airport
in his Franciscan car. 6 days in New York.
     The Benefit would be for Conscientization.
"Not for any institution!" Tony told me. *Not for any institution.*
I didn't get a window seat. As we took off, out in the distance
     (just a glimpse)
the silhouette of skyscrapers against a sky filled with automobile
    exhaust
     acids and carbon monoxide.

1973   [J. C.]

EPISTLE TO MONSIGNOR CASALDÁLIGA

Monsignor:
I read that in a sacking by the Military Police
in the Prelature of São Félix, they carried off, among
other things, the Portuguese translation (I didn't
know there was one) of *Psalms* by Ernesto Cardenal. And
that all those arrested were given electric shocks
for Psalms that many had perhaps not read.
I have suffered for them, and for so many others, in
   "the nets of death" . . . "the snares of the Abyss"
    My brothers and sisters
with the goad at your breasts, with the goad at your penis.
I will tell you: those Psalms have been banned here too
and Somoza said a short while ago in a speech
that he would eradicate the "obscurantism" of Solentiname.

I saw your picture on the banks of the Araguaia
the day of your consecration, with your miter
which as we know is a palm-leaf hat
and your crozier, an oar from the Amazonia. And I've learned
that you're now waiting to be sentenced by the Military Court.
I imagine you, while waiting, smiling as in the picture (smiling not
at the camera but at all that was to come)
at the hour when the woods turn greener
or sadder,
   in the distance the lovely water of the Araguaia,
   the sun sinking behind distant estates.
The forest begins there, "its silence like a deafness."
I spent a week on the Amazon (Leticia) and I remember
the banks of trees hidden by tangles of parasites
like finance companies.
   At night you've heard their strange noises
(some are like moans and others like cackles).
Jaguar after tapir, tapir frightening the monkeys, the monkeys
scaring off . . .
    macaws?

(it's on a page of Humboldt)
   like a class society.
An evening melancholy like that of the courtyards of
      penitentiary nuns.
In the air there is dampness, and a kind of DEOPS smell . . .
Perhaps a sad wind blows from the Northeast
         from the sad Northeast . . .
There is a black frog in the black *igarapés*
(I've read) a black frog that asks: *What
forr? What
forr?*

Perhaps a flying fish leaps up. A heron takes flight, as graceful
as Miss Brazil.
         In spite of the companies, the enterprises. The beauty
of those shores, a prelude to the society that we shall have.
That we shall have. They cannot, even though they try,
         take a planet away from the celestial system.

Is Anaconda around there? Is
Kennecott?
Off there, like here, the people are afraid.
The laymen, you've written,
         "through the jungle like jaguars, like birds"
I've learned the name of a boy (Chico)
and the name of a girl (Rosa)
               The tribe is moving upstream.
The Companies come putting up fences. Across
the Mato Grosso sky move the landowners in their private planes.
And they don't invite you to the big barbecue with the Minister of
      the Interior.
               The Companies sowing desolation.
They bring in the telegraph to transmit false news.
The transistor to the poor, for murmured lies.
         Truth is forbidden for it makes you free.
Desolation and division and barbed wire.
You're a poet and you write metaphors. But you've also written:
               "slavery is not a metaphor."
And they penetrate even into the upper Xingú,
the hunters of usurious bank concessions.
         Weeping in those regions like the Amazonian rain.
The Military Police have told you that all

the Church should worry about is "souls"
But what about children starved by corporations?

Perhaps it's the middle of the night in the Prelature of São Félix.
You alone, in the Mission house, surrounded by jungle,
the jungle through which the corporations come advancing. It's
the hour of the DEOPS spies and the gunmen of the Companies.
    Is that a friend at the door or is it the Death Squadron?

I imagine (if there's a moon) a melancholy Amazonia moon
    its light shines on private property.
The great estate not for farming, let's get this straight,
but so that the little farmer won't have his little farm.

The middle of the night. "Brother, how long will it take to reach
Paranará?" "We don't know, brother.
We don't know if we're near or far away
or if we've already passed it. But let's row, brother."

The middle of the night. The little lights
of the dispossessed shine on the shores.
    Their tearful reflections.
Far, far away laugh the lights of Rio de Janeiro
and the lights of Brasilia.

How *shall they possess the earth* if the earth is owned by landowners?
Unproductive, prized only for land
speculation and fat loans from the Bank of Brazil.
    There He is always sold for Thirty Dollars
      on the River of the Dead.
    The price of a peon. In spite of
    2,000 years of inflation.

The middle of the night. There is a humble little light (I don't know
just where)
    a leper colony on the Amazon
the lepers are there on the dock
waiting for Che's raft to come back.

I've noticed that you quote my *Homage to the American Indians*
I'm surprised that the book should travel as far as the upper Xingú
where you, Monsignor, defend these Indians. What greater homage!

I think of the Pataxó Indians poisoned with smallpox.
   of 10,000 Long-Ribbons, only 500 now.
The Tapaiamas receiving gifts of sugar with arsenic.
Another Mato Grosso tribe dynamited from a Cessna.
The harsh *mangaré* drum does not sound calling to the moon dancers,
the dancers disguised as butterflies, chewing the mystic coca leaf,
the naked girls painted with the symbolic markings
of the boa's skin, with gourd rattles on their ankles
around the Tree of Life (the *pifayo* palm).
A chain of diamond shapes represents the serpent, and inside
each diamond other frets, each fret another serpent.
So that there are many serpents in the body of a single one:
The communal organization of many individuals. Plurality
within unity.
       At the beginning there was only water and sky.
       All was a void, all was great night.
Afterward He made mountains, rivers. He said: "now everything
  is there."
The rivers called one another by their names.
    Men used to be howling monkeys.
The earth has the shape of the breadfruit tree.
    All that time there was a ladder to climb up to the sky.
Columbus found them in Cuba in a paradise where everything was
  held in common.
"The earth common like the sun and the water, without
  meum et tuum."
They gave someone a length of cloth and cutting it into equal pieces
he divided it among the whole tribe.
No tribe in America with private property, that I know of.
    The whites brought money
the private monetary evaluation of things.
      (Shouts . . . the crackling of huts in flames . . .
       shots)
Of 19,000 Muducuras, 1,200. Of 4,000 Carajás, 400.
The Tapalumas, completely gone.
The private appropriation of Eden
or the Green Hell.
As a Jesuit has written:
       "the thirst for blood greater than the River."

  A new order. Or rather
  a new heaven and a new earth.

New Jerusalem. Neither New York nor Brasilia.
A passion for change: the nostalgia
of that city. A beloved community.
        We are foreigners in Consumer City.
The new man, and not the new Oldsmobile.

Idols are idealism. While the prophets
were professing dialectical materialism.
Idealism: Miss Brazil on the screen blotting out
100,000 prostitutes on the streets of São Paulo.

And in the futuristic Brasilia the decrepit marshals
from their desks execute handsome young men by telephone
        exterminate the happy tribe with a telegram
trembling, rheumatic and arthritic, cadaverous,
backed up by fat gangsters with dark glasses.

This morning the termite entered my cabin
on the side where the books are (Fanon, Freire . . .
also Plato): a perfect society
but without one change
        for millions of years without one change.
Not long ago a reporter asked me why I write poetry:
for the same reason as Amos, Nahum, Ageo, Jeremiah . . .
You have written: "Cursed be private property."
And Saint Basil: "Owners of the common goods
because they were the first to seize them."
For Communists there is no God, only justice.
For Christians there is no God without justice.
Monsignor, we are subversives
a secret code on a card in a file who knows where,
followers of the ill-clad and visionary proletariat, a professional
agitator, executed for conspiring against the System.
It was, you know, a torture intended for subversives,
the cross was for political criminals, not a cluster of rubies
on a bishop's breast.
            Nothing is profane any more.
He is not beyond the atmospheric skies.
What does it matter, Monsignor, if the Military Police or the CIA
converts us into food for the bacteria in the soil
and scatters us throughout the universe.
        Pilate stuck the sign up in 4 languages: SUBVERSIVE.

One arrested in the bakery.
Another one waiting for a bus to go to work.
A long-haired boy falls in a São Paulo street.
            There is resurrection of the flesh. If not
how can there be a permanent Revolution?
One day *El Tiempo* appeared jubilant on the streets of Bogotá
(it reached me even in Solentiname) CAMILO TORRES DEAD
            enormous black letters
and he's more alive than ever defying *El Tiempo*.

And they say in Brasilia:
"Do not picture for us true visions, speak to us
of flattering things, contemplate illusions."
            The Brazilian miracle
            of a Hilton Hotel surrounded by hovels.
The price of things goes up
            and the price of people comes down.
Manpower as cheap as is possible (cleanliness
is not for them . . . the Beethoven Symphony).
And in the Northeast then stomachs are devouring themselves.
Yes, Julião, capital is multiplying like bacilli.
Capitalism, the accumulation of sin, like the pollution
of São Paulo
            the whiskey-colored miasma over São Paulo.
Its cornerstone is inequality.
In the Amazon I met a famous Mike
who exported piranhas to the U.S.A.
and he could send only two in each tank,
so that one could always elude the other:
if there are three or more they all destroy one another.
That's like this Brazilian model of piranhas.
            Mass production of misery, crime
            in industrial quantities. Death
            on the production line.
Mario-Japa asked for water on the *pau-de-arara*
and they made him swallow a pound of salt.
With no news because of censorship, we know only:
there where the helicopters gather is the Body of Christ.
About violence, I would say:
            there exists the violence of Evolution
            and the violence that retards Evolution.
(And a love stronger than the DEOPS and the Death Squadron.)

But
    sadism and masochism are class harmony
    sadism and masochism of oppressor and oppressed.
But love also is implacable (like the DEOPS).
The yearning for union can carry one to the *pau-de-arara,* to
the machine-gun-butt slams on the head, the
punches in the face with bandaged fists, the electrodes.
    For that love many have been castrated.
You feel the loneliness of being only individuals.
Perhaps while I'm writing you you've already been condemned.
Perhaps later I'll be jailed.
Prophet there where the Araguaia and the Xingú come together
and also poet
    you are the voice of people with adhesive tape across
    their mouths
        This is no time for literary criticism.
Nor for attacking the gorillas with surrealistic poems.
And what use are metaphors if slavery is not a metaphor,
if death in the River of the Dead is not a metaphor,
if the Squadron of Death is not?
    Now the people weep on the *pau-de-arara.*
But every rooster that crows in the Brazilian night
is now subversive
    it crows "Revolucião"
and it's subversive, at the end of each night,
like a girl handing out leaflets or posters about Che,
    each red dawn.

Greetings to the farmers, the peons, the laymen in the jungle,
to the *tapurapé* chief, the Little Sisters of Foucauld, Chico, and
    Rosa.

With a hug from
    Ernesto Cardenal

1974   [D. D. W.]

EPISTLE TO JOSÉ CORONEL URTECHO

Poet:
I have enjoyed your "Lectures on Private Enterprise"
(Homilies, I would say) which you wrote in Granada, in your little
     house on the lake, and you took
so long to write them that you thought—you told me there once—
     that perhaps when
you finished them there would be no private enterprise.
       There still is. But there won't be for very long.
Yours was a heroic effort to be understood,
in spite of the inflation and devaluation of language
in the language of every day, which is also that of poetry,
by the entrepreneurs. And it was, I suppose,
a futile effort. They will not be saved, save
       the exceptions we know.
Some will be saved individually.
        Engels was a millionaire.
       You know as well as I that they are lost cases.
       Save a few whom we know about.
(A revolutionary become entrepreneur to finance *Das Kapital* . . .)
You, poet, who as you say possess no "earthly goods,"
and often repeat to us that Las Brisas ranch is not yours
but María's and your children's and that you are staying there only
     as a guest,
       and never in your life have you sold anything,
have now preached about Private Enterprise. And it was,
       it seems to me, only so that those who looked would not see,
        those who heard would not understand
  "unless they are converted and saved"
. . . a Cadillac through the eye of a needle.
They may be good people, according to Marx. Some capitalists have
a good heart. So: it's not a question of changing the heart
       but the system.

Private property—that euphemism.
     "Thieves" is not rhetoric.

It's not a figure of speech.
Charity in the Bible is *sedagah* (justice)
 (the correct terminology that maestro Pound required)
and "alms," a giving back.
This has much to do with inflation and devaluation
   (of language and of money).
The solution is simple: to give to others in brotherhood.
   Capitalism impedes communion.
   Banks impede communion.
And no one with more than he really needs.
It's in the banks' interest that language be confused
maestro Pound has taught us
therefore our task is to make language clear.
To revalue words for the new nation
while the FSLN advances in the north.
Saint Ambrose thundered in his Milan cathedral, on the threshold
of feudalism, the cathedral not yet Gothic
or Romanesque but revolutionary:
 THE EARTH BELONGS TO EVERYBODY, NOT THE RICH
and Saint John Chrysostom in Byzantium with his Biblical Marxism:
"the community of goods is more faithful to nature."
In the language of the New Testament, I was saying to you back
   there
in Las Brisas, citing Father Segundo,
  the "sin" is conservatism.
The world in Saint John is the status quo.
The world-sin is the system.
A change of *attitude* is one of structures.
   Acquire more earnings to
   accumulate more capital to
   acquire more earnings to
    and so on to infinity.
Others'. The work of others according to Chrysostom.
"I enjoy my things . . ." "No, not yours
but those of others."
A kind of automatic fruition. So many times already
we have commented on this, with the texts of maestro Pound.
   The "parthenogenesis" of money.
And the girls of Matiguá are very beautiful
but they are being sterilized.

There still is private property. But there won't be for very long.
   This prehistory is already passing

from the surface of this planet in the hands of a few.
We were reading the other afternoon here under the mango tree
looking at the blue lake and across it the little island La Cigüeña
what Fidel says: "the earth will be like the air"
and the young people of the Youth Club are already dreaming of
    that day
when the island La Cigüeña, La Venada, all the islands
are theirs, and the whole country. "Abroad
one says 'my land,' " Laureano said, "but it's a lie,
it belongs to other sons of bitches."
And we have learned that now in Portugal
the bankers are in prison.
        Millionaires, and not shoeshine boys.
The Bank of the Holy Spirit has been closed.
A kind of automatic fruition, as if
money labored.
        The holy banking business . . .
        Its function is to look for money that doesn't exist
and lend it.
        There is no communion with God or with
        man if there are classes,
            if there is exploitation
        there is no communion.
They've told me I talk only about politics now.
It's not about politics but about Revolution
which for me is the same thing as the kingdom of God.

        Building the earth.
The transformation of the earth into a human earth
or the humanization of nature.
Everything, even the heavens, a little man, as Vallejo said.
        Filling this blue planet with love.
        (Or the revolution is bureaucratic).
Like the step from australopithecus to pithecanthropus.
The subject fully objective
and the object fully subjective.
        Masters of nature and of themselves,
          free, without a State.

Ursa Major then will have the form of a giraffe.
The new man is not just one,
you told me one day there on the river,
        he is many together.

"A change in man," they say, not in structures. But
a change in structures is also one in man's subconscious!
       A new relationship among men
       and between man and the natural world
       and with the Other
          (on which you also insist so much)
Marx said he did not know
       what there would be after communism.

As the tree opens toward the light
evolution opens toward love.
The planet will not be dominated by insects, monkeys or robots
       or by Frankenstein's monster.
A trillion and some since the first cell . . .
He saw that matter was good (a materialistic God).
And with creation began liberation.
       And sin is counter-evolutionary
the tendency toward the inorganic
       is antihistorical.
How did our matter escape from antimatter?
And what does Christ's giving the kingdom to the Father mean?
. . . Who was revealed in the bush as He Who Hears the Masses
   as the liberation from slave society.
And we might also wonder: what relationship is there
between resurrection and the means of production?
       All cells come from other cells.
Life is produced by the participation of life.
       Reproduction is by communion.
It would be unjust, the final injustice, if there were none.
       There is resurrection, if not,
could those who died before the revolution not then be freed?
The abolition of death . . . But first naturally
       that of money.

You have returned to the river, to Las Brisas ranch
which isn't yours but María's and your children's,
to your monastery in the Medio Queso plains surrounded by jungle
which is always covered with water except in summer
where a short time back a president without a bodyguard visited you,
not Nicaragua's of course, Costa Rica's.
Your monastery where you now practice your painful penitence
of writing prose. Your painful daily prose.
But prophetic prose.

I prefer verse, you know, because it's easier
             and briefer
and the people understand it better, like posters.
                              Without forgetting that
     "revolutionary art without artistic value
      has no revolutionary value"   (Mao)
You were a reactionary before
and now you are "uncomfortable" in the left
but in the extreme left,
without having changed anything inside you;
the reality around you has changed.
The prophet can make mistakes. Jeremiah
—I have learned—was wrong in a prophecy on international politics.
You, poet, have returned to your remote monastery
              (now threatened by an Onassis oil pipeline,
like Solentiname the chain of Howard Hughes' casinos)
              and you hold forth there at all hours facing the plains
for anyone willing to listen to you, prophesying at all hours,
              money as the end of life
         work for the love of money and not for the love of work
facing the plains, always green even in summer, with
palm trees, *cubas rousseauneanas* and *patacona* doves
and *poponé* doves and squawking flocks of whistling ducks
              the Jesuit's university, INCAE,
         the realists with no more reality than what produces earnings,
and from time to time *martín-peñas* also fly by
and kingfishers with long beaks and tangled topknots
and *veteranos* with plucked necks also in flocks
              the young executive with no time to have his wife
                   or the friends in Managua
              who never do anything because they are too busy
or they are *guairones,* or the plane from San José, Costa Rica,
which is now coming down to land at Los Chiles, or they are
         cormorants
              the two kinds of people who run things in Nicaragua
              the bloodsuckers / and the shiteaters,
and the coot the color of a waterflower runs
along the ditchwater, and the black *sargento*
emerges from the *sorocontiles* with his bloodstain like a national
         guard,
              the Shitocracy,
generals and businessmen, when they are not businessmen-generals,
in your rustic study built by María, open on the plain

far off on the horizon the blue line of the river nearly invisible
and from time to time nearly inaudible the murmur of a boat's motor
                    Nicaraguan history stopped in 1936
and if it is late the macaws pass by in pairs, a *cuaco* sings
who knows where, the frog croaks "you" calling the female
"you, you, you," and when the female comes to him he mounts her.
    He's crazy, but since they all obey him, he seems sane!
The heron of foamy feathers and yellow beak takes flight
and the moon comes out, the full moon on the Medio Queso plain
and María calls us for supper.

"Revolutionary art without artistic value . . ."
            And artistic art without revolutionary value? It seems to me
that great bards of the 20th century are in Publicity
        those Keatses and Shelleys singing the Colgate smile
Cosmic Coca-Cola, the pause that refreshes,
        the make of car that will take us to the land of happiness.
The inflation and devaluation of language
keeping pace with that of money and caused by the same people.
            They call plunder investments.
And they're covering the earth with empty cans.
        Like a river in Cleveland which is now flammable
language, also polluted.
            "It appears that he (Johnson) never understood
            that words also have a real meaning
            besides serving for propaganda"
            Time said that he does understand it and he lies just the
                same.
And the defoliation of Vietnam
is a Resource Control Program
it's also a defoliation of language.
            And language avenges itself refusing to communicate.
            Plunder: investments
There are also crimes of the CIA in the realm of semantics.
Here in Nicaragua, as you have said:
the language of the government and private enterprise
against the language of the Nicaraguan people.

I remember that time in the little port of San Carlos
where one turns to go to the post office and telegraph station
and one sees the great open sky-colored lake, and Solentiname
also sky-colored, and the volcanoes of Costa Rica
and the sunsets are comparable only to those of Naples

according to Squier:
the national guardsman drunk on the sidewalk with his Garand
        pointing straight into his mouth
                leaning on his Garand so as not to fall,
the worker drunk lying in the mud of the street
                covered with flies and with his fly open.
And so you told me: "This must be written in a poem
    so that they can know later what Somoza was."
(Poetry as a poster
                or a documentary film
                or a news item.)
You were with the reaction before. But your "reaction"
was not so much the return to the Middle Ages as to the Stone Age
(or perhaps even farther back?)
                I have had a nostalgia for paradise all my life
                I have looked for it like a Guaraní
but now I know it's not in the past
(a scientific error in the Bible which Christ has corrected)
but in the future.

You are an incorrigible optimist, like me, and
at least for the short term you are more so than I am,
and you turn on the radio each morning to hear the news that
        Somoza fell.
Now you are going to be 70
and I hope you won't fall into the temptation of pessimism.
Revolution doesn't end in this world
                you told me once on this island, facing the lake
and communism will continue in heaven.
        The FSLN is advancing in the north.
Even in the Jesuits' university there are signs of life,
the tenacious grass again shows itself among the concrete,
        the tender grass cracks through the concrete.
Your lectures will be more appreciated without private enterprise.
Right here I am looking through the fishnet at the calm lake, and
        I think:
            as the blue lake reflects the celestial atmosphere
            so will be the kingdom of heaven on this planet.
            A heron by the water takes communion with a sardine.
Regards to María and to the river.
A hug from
            Ernesto Cardenal

1975   [P. W. B.]

LIGHTS

That top-secret flight at night.
We might have been shot down. The night calm and clear.
The sky teeming, swarming with stars. The Milky Way
so bright behind the thick pane of the window,
        a sparkling white mass in the black night
with its millions of evolutionary and revolutionary changes.
We were going over the water to avoid Somoza's air force,
        but close to the coast.
The small plane flying low, and flying slowly.
First the lights of Rivas, taken and retaken by Sandinists,
        now almost in Sandinist hands.
Then other lights: Granada, in the hands of the Guard
                    (it would be attacked that night).
Masaya, completely liberated. So many fell there.
Farther out a bright glow: Managua. Site of so many battles.
(The Bunker.) Still the stronghold of the Guard.
Diriamba, liberated. Jinotepe, fighting it out. So much heroism
glitters in those lights. Montelimar—the pilot shows us—:
the tyrant's estate near the sea. Puerto Somoza, next to it.
The Milky Way above, and the lights of Nicaragua's revolution.
Out there, in the north, I think I see Sandino's campfire.
        ("That light is Sandino.")
The stars above us, and the smallness of this land
but also its importance, these
tiny lights of men. I think: everything is light.
The planet comes from the sun. It is light turned solid.
This plane's electricity is light. Its metal is light. The warmth
    of life comes from the sun.
                "Let there be light."
There is also darkness.
There are strange reflections—I don't know where they come
    from—on the clear surface of the windows.
A red glow: the tail lights of the plane.
And reflections on the calm sea: they must be stars.
I look at the light from my cigarette—it also comes from the sun,
    from a star.

And the outline of a great ship. The U.S. aircraft carrier
sent to patrol the Pacific coast?
A big light on our right startles us. A jet attacking?
No. The moon coming out, a half-moon, so peaceful, lit by the sun.
    The danger of flying on such a clear night.
And suddenly the radio. Jumbled words filling the small plane.
The Guard? The pilot says: "It's our side."
          They're on our wavelengths.
Now we're close to León, the territory liberated.
A burning reddish-orange light, like the red-hot tip of a cigar:
    Corinto:
the powerful lights of the docks flickering on the sea.
And now at last the beach at Poneloya, and the plane coming in
        to land,
the string of foam along the coast gleaming in the moonlight.
    The plane coming down. A smell of insecticide.
And Sergio tells me: "The smell of Nicaragua!"
It's the most dangerous moment, enemy aircraft
          may be waiting for us over this airport.
And the airport lights at last.
We've landed. From out of the dark come olive-green-clad comrades
to greet us with hugs.
We feel their warm bodies, that also come from the sun,
that also are light.
          This revolution is fighting the darkness.
It was daybreak on July 18th. And the beginning
        of all that was about to come.

1979   [J. C.]

First printed in a limited edition by the Black Hole School of Poethnics,
welcoming Nicaragua's new Ambassador to the United Nations, H. E.
Víctor Tinoco, at the United Nations Church Center, October 17, 1979,
año de la liberación.

IDENTIFICATIONS

I have not attempted to define all the Nicaraguan birds and other animals mentioned, or untranslatable names of foods, or Nicaraguan place names that could be defined only as "a place in Nicaragua."
—D. D. W.

Acahualinca: the slum area of Managua, capital of Nicaragua, and site of footprints of prehistoric men and animals fleeing a volcanic eruption.

Adelita: "Si Adelita se fuera con otro . . ." was a popular marching song of the Mexican revolutionary armies, 1910–17.

Ageo: Aggeus or Haggi, a 6th-century B.C. prophet, and the Old Testament book that bears his name.

Altamirano, Pedrón (–1937): a Sandino commander beheaded by National Guardsmen.

Araguaia: Brazilian river that empties into the Paraná.

Arnold, Kenneth: a former editor of The Johns Hopkins University Press, now with Trinity University Press.

Auden, Wystan Hugh (1907–73): an English poet and playwright who lived many years in New York City.

Baez, Joan (1941–): an American folk singer and antiwar activist.

Báez Bone, Adolfo: a close friend of Cardenal who was captured in an abortive plot and tortured to death.

Bashan cows: a reference to Amos 4:1: "Hear this word, ye kine of Bashan . . . which oppress the poor, which crush the needy, which say to their masters: Bring, and let us drink."

Basil: Saint Basil or Basilius the Great (329–79), Bishop of Caesarea in Asia Minor and one of the four Fathers of the Greek Church.

Berrigan, Daniel (1921–): an American Jesuit priest, poet, and political activist. Jailed for having destroyed some Selective Service files, he was paroled in 1972.

Berrigan, Philip Francis (1923–): an American Catholic priest and political activist. Jailed for having destroyed some Selective Service files, he was paroled in 1972.

Blanchart, Father: a French Marxist Dominican monk.

Bomba: nickname of King Ferdinand II of the Two Sicilies (1810–59). He acquired the nickname by bombing Messina in 1848 and Palermo in 1849.

Bryan-Chamorro Treaty: in 1916 it gave the United States an option for an alternative canal between the Atlantic and the Pacific.

Buitrago, Julio César (1949–69): a member of the FSLN, killed in a shootout with the National Guard.

cadejo: a fantastic animal that roams the streets at night and pursues drunkards.

Camilo: either Camilo Cienfuegos or Camilo Torres.

campesino: literally one who lives in the campo (countryside). Most campesinos are farmworkers, but some are fishermen.

Carías Andino, Tiburcio (1876–1969): dictator of Honduras, 1939–49, "the dictator who didn't build the greatest number of miles of railroad" ("Zero Hour").

Castillo Armas, Colonel Carlos (–1957): in 1954, with U.S. support, he overthrew the government of Guatemalan leftist President Jacobo Arbenz Guzmán. He was assassinated three years later.

Castro, Fidel (1926–): Cuba's revolutionary leader.

chachalaca: chatterbox, a perching bird with a chattering cry.

Che: Ernesto (Che) Guevara (1927–67): an Argentine doctor who became Castro's chief lieutenant. He left Cuba to carry the revolution to other countries, tried to foster a peasant revolt in Bolivia, was captured and shot.

Chrysostom: Saint John Chrysostom (347–407), patriarch of Constantinople.

Cienfuegos, Camilo (–1959): a tailor who became one of Castro's chief lieutenants. He died in a seaplane crash.

Clement of Alexandria (150–215): Greek theologian of the early Christian Church, founder of the Alexandrian school of theology.

conscientization: learning to perceive social, political, and economic contradictions, and taking action against oppression.

Corita: see Kent, Corita.

Coronel Urtecho, José (1904–): Nicaraguan poet and essayist.

Cortés, Alfonso: a mad Nicaraguan poet whom Cardenal knew as a young man and whose poetry was translated by Thomas Merton.

Cullen, Michael: an Irish-American pacifist who burned his draft card and some Selective Service files in Milwaukee.

Dalton, Roque (1933–75): a Salvadorean poet who lived in Cuba for a time but went back to El Salvador to fight (and die) for freedom.

Darío, Rubén (1867–1916): Nicaragua's first great poet, founder of *modernismo* and the most influential Hispanic poet of his time.

Day, Dorothy (1897–): editor of *The Catholic Worker*.

Dean, John Wesley III (1938–): a former White House counsel.

DEOPS: the Brazilian Secret Police.

Díaz, Adolfo: Nicaraguan Provisional President who in 1912 invited the U.S. Marines to land in Nicaragua to maintain order.

Engels, Friedrich (1820–95): a wealthy German socialist, co-founder (with Marx) of modern communism.

English, Jack: a Cleveland journalist who became a cook at *The Catholic Worker* and later a monk.

Estrada Cabrera, Manuel (1857–1924): Guatemalan President, 1898–1905, and dictator, 1905–20.

Ezra: see Pound, Ezra.

Fanon, Frantz Omar (1925–61): a French West Indian psychologist, leader of the Algerian National Front. Author of *Black Skin, White Masks* (1952) and *The Wretched of the Earth* (1961).

Fidel: see Castro, Fidel.

Forest, Jim: a pacifist and ex-monk who was a friend of Merton.

Freire, Paulo: a Brazilian political exile and leftist Catholic, creator of a revolutionary method of training for literacy, author of *Educación del oprimido* ("The Pedagogy of the Oppressed").

FSLN: Frente Sandinista de Liberación Nacional, the guerrilla movement that overthrew Somoza in 1979.

Gage, Thomas (–1656): an English traveler, author of *English-American: His Travel by Sea and Land* (1648).

Genie, Samuel: former Director of Internal Security of the Nicaraguan Guardia Nacional.

Gertrude, Saint (1256–1311): a German, known as Gertrude the Great, famed for supernatural visions.

Hafiz (1320–89): a Persian poet.

Hennacy, Ammon: a war protestor, author of the autobiography, *The Book of Ammon*.

Hernández Martínez, Maximiliano (1882–1966): pro-fascist dictator of El Salvador, 1931–44.

Hughes, Howard Robard (1905–76): an eccentric and elusive American billionaire.

Hugo, Victor (1803–85): a French poet, playwright, and novelist.

igarapé: a Guaraní word for canoe path, applied to a system of canals that border the Amazon.

Juan Potosme: a name invented by Cardenal for the average poor man.

Kent, Corita (1918–): an American painter and serigrapher, formerly a nun.

La Porte, Roger: an antiwar protester who burned himself to death at the age of twenty-two in front of the United Nations.

latifundista: a big landowner.

Laughlin, James IV (1914–): a poet, publisher of New Directions, youthful disciple of Ezra Pound, friend and publisher of Merton and Cardenal.

Lee, William A.: a lieutenant in Company M of the Nicaraguan Guardia Nacional, and the subject of many atrocity stories.

leprocomio: *leprosorio* (leper colony).

Managua: capital of Nicaragua, and one of its lakes. On December 23, 1972, much of the city was destroyed by a series of earthquakes that killed 10,000, injured another 15,000, and left homeless half the 183,000 residents.

Maurin, Peter: editor of *The Catholic Worker*.

McAllister, Elizabeth: a former nun who married Philip Berrigan while she was in prison. She was convicted of smuggling mail out of prison, but the conviction was overturned in 1972.

mel et lac sub lingua tua: milk and honey under your tongue.

Merton, Thomas (1915–68): an American poet-priest under whose guidance Cardenal was for a time a Trappist novice.

Moncada, José María (1868–1945): President of Nicaragua, 1929–32, opponent of Sandino. Faced with U.S. intervention in 1932, he declared martial law.

Moore, Marianne Craig (1887–1972): an American poet, winner of a Pultizer Prize in 1952.

moskitos: the Mosquito or Miskito Indians who live on the east coast of Nicaragua and Honduras. From 1860 to 1894 this area was the autonomous Mosquito Kingdom.

Nahum: a minor prophet of the 7th century B.C., and the book of the Bible that bears his name.

Nicanor: see Parra, Nicanor.

1936: "Nicaraguan history ended in 1936." Anastasio Somoza García seized power in 1937.

Niquinohomo: the home town of the Nicaraguan hero Sandino.

O'Hara, Frank (1926–66): a leading poet of the New York School, curator of the Museum of Modern Art, author of *Lunch Poems*.

Ortez y Guillén, Miguel Angel (–1931): a Sandino commander who sometimes used "General Ferrara" as a *nom de guerre*. Killed in action.

Oviedo, Gonzalo Fernández de (1478–1557): author of *Historia natural y general de las Indias* (1535).

Pablo Antonio: Pablo Antonio Cuadra (1912–), a Nicaraguan poet and editor and a relative of Cardenal.

Paranará: a Brazilian-like name invented by Cardenal.

Parra, Nicanor (1914–): a Chilean poet and physicist, author of *Poems and Antipoems* (1954) and *Emergency Poems* (1972), both published by New Directions.

Pasos, Joaquín (1915–1947): Nicaraguan vanguard poet.

pau-de-arara: an iron bar from which prisoners were hung head down.

Popol Vuh: a huge collection of Mayan myths, written in Quiché.

Potosme: see Juan Potosme.

Pound, Ezra Loomis (1885–1972): a poet, critic, editor, and translator. A major influence on English and American literature, and on Cardenal and Laughlin.

quetzal: the national bird of Nicaragua.

Randall, Margaret (1936–): a U.S.-born resident of Cuba, poet, editor, and translator.

Rubén: see Darío, Rubén.

Rugama, Leonel: a 20-year-old poet and seminary student who became a member of FSLN. He was killed in a shootout.

Sandino, Augusto César (1895–1934): a Nicaraguan guerrilla leader who fought, 1927–32, against the intervention of the U.S. Marines. He was assassinated in Managua on the night of February 21.

Sandino, Sócrates (–1934): half-brother of Augusto, under whom he served and with whom he was assassinated on the night of February 21.

Sierra Maestra: a chain of mountains in Cuba's Oriente Province, the scene of Castro's first victories.

Sitwell, Dame Edith (1887–1964): an English poet, critic, and novelist.

Solentiname, Nuestra Señora de: Father Cardenal's commune on Lake Nicaragua, destroyed by Somoza's troops in October 1977.

Somoza Debayle, Anastasio (Tachito) (1925–): a son of Anastasio Somoza García and President of Nicaragua, 1967–79, now in exile.

Somoza García, Anastasio (Tacho) (1896–1956): Commander of the Nicaraguan National Guard, he seized power in 1937 and ruled the country until his assassination.

Spencer, Mister: a Canadian millionaire mine owner in Nicaragua.

Spender, Stephen (1909–): an English poet and critic.

Squier, Ephraim George (1821–88): an American archeologist, author of *Nicaragua* (1852).

Stimson, Henry Lewis, 1867–1950: U.S. Secretary of War, 1911–13; Presidential Delegate to Nicaragua, 1927; Secretary of State, 1929–33; Secretary of War, 1940–45.

TACA: Transportes Aéreos de Centro América.

Torres, Camilo (–1966): Colombian guerrilla priest, killed in action.

tupamaros: Uruguayan revolutionary underground movement.

Ubico Castañeda, Jorge (1878–1946): military dictator of Guatemala, 1931–44.

Umanzor, Juan Pablo (–1934): a Sandino general, assassinated with him on February 21.

Vallejo, César (1895–1938): a Peruvian Marxist, political exile, and one of the great Hispanic poets of this century.

Vanderbilt, Cornelius (Commodore) (1794–1877): the founder of the family fortune and owner of a shipping line to California via Nicaragua, 1851–58.

Veronese, Vittorino: President of Catholic Action and also of the Bank of Rome.

Walker, William (1824–60): a U.S. adventurer who in 1856 captured Granada in Nicaragua and became President. Vanderbilt forced him to flee the country. He was captured and shot on one of his many attempts to return.

Washington Place: a street in Greenwich Village in New York City.

Welles, Sumner (1892–1961): a U.S. diplomat, Under-Secretary of State, 1937–42.

Williams, Tennessee (1914–): an American playwright, awarded a Pulitzer Prize in 1947.

Zavala, Don Manuel: an aged Nicaraguan whom Cardenal knew in New York City.

Zemurray, Samuel (1877–1961): a Turkish-American fruit importer who sold his company to United Fruit. He thereby became its largest stockholder and its president.